Digest of
BUSINESS
LAW

Digest of
BUSINESS
LAW
SECOND EDITION

WILLIS W. HAGEN
University of Wisconsin
Milwaukee

GORDON H. JOHNSON
University of Wisconsin
Madison

WEST PUBLISHING COMPANY
St. Paul • New York • Los Angeles • San Francisco

COPYRIGHT © 1979 By WEST PUBLISHING CO.
50 West Kellogg Boulevard
P.O. Box 3526
St. Paul, Minnesota 55165

Printed in the United States of America

Library of Congress Cataloging in Publication Data

Hagen, Willis W.
  Digest of business law.

   1.   Business law—United States.   I.   Johnson,
Gordon H., joint author.   II.   Title.
HF889.3.H26 1979   346'.73'07   79-11798
ISBN 0-8299-0261-9
1st Reprint—1980

Preface

Digest of Business Law is designed to present to the reader a concise and comprehensive treatment of the law of business. The aim of the authors is to combine thoroughness with brevity and provide students of the law with a convenient way to master basic legal knowledge.

In planning the book, the authors perceived several needs which they hope it will serve. Present available texts, quite properly, consist of lengthy presentations of a wide variety of subject matter and extensive quotations from cases and statutes. A need for a supplementary text, which digests the subject matter, seems indicated. As a condensation of the law, the book should prove useful to the student both for a better comprehension of the more expanded materials and for periodic review.

Law lectures characteristically impose a substantial burden on students with respect to note taking. Often the notes, while concise, do not accurately record the lecturer's presentation. *Digest of Business Law* may be used as a lecture outline, available to students assuring that the main thrust of the material presented is properly preserved for study.

A special effort was made by the authors to assure that this book would provide adequate coverage of the subject matter of CPA Business Law examinations. Their experience with CPA law review courses goes back many years, and they feel that the book is an appropriate text for such courses and for independent preparation for CPA certification.

Short courses in business law, where time does not allow leisurely contemplation of legal thought, may employ the book as a useful learning tool. It may be supplemented with the teacher's experiences and perhaps some outside reading of reported cases.

Learning the law is enhanced by several inputs: lectures, textual material, outside reading, and case and problem discussions, all of which make a contribution to the student's understanding in different ways. *Digest of Business Law* can serve as a medium for the synthesis of the study of the legal aspects of business administration.

v

Chapter Cross-Index

	Smith & Roberson 4th Edition	Lusk, et al 4th Edition	Anderson & Kumpf 7th Edition U.C.C.	Corley & Robert 11th Edition	Howell, Allison & Jentz	Wyatt & Wyatt 6th Edition	Clarkson, Miller & Blaire
Part One: Law and Governmental Regulation							
1 Introduction to Law	1-2	1-2	1-2	1-4	1-6	1-2	1-2
2 Crimes and Torts	1	3-5	3-4	5-6	7	3	3-4
3 Antitrust Law	37	50-53	5	40	44-46	49	50-51
Part Two: Contracts							
4 Introduction	3	6	9	7	8	4	5
5 Agreement	3	7-8	10	8	9	5	6
6 Genuineness of Assent	4	9	12	10	13	9	10
7 Consideration	5	10	13	9	10	6	7
8 Capacity of Parties	7	11	11	10	11	7	8
9 Legality of Object	6	12	14	11	12	8	9
10 Writing Requirements	8-9	13	15-16	12	14	10	11

11	Rights of Third Parties	10	14	17	13	15	11	12
12	Performance	12	15	19	14	16	12-13	13-14
13	Discharge	11	15	18	15	16	14	13
Part Three:	Guaranty, Suretyship and Insurance							
14	Guaranty and Suretyship	-	44	35	26	-	59	31
15	Insurance	46	-	36-37	-	-	58	54
Part Four:	Employment and Agency							
16	Employment	13	20	42	30	-	50	33, 47
17	The Agency Relation	13	16	39	32	29	33, 36	33
18	Rights and Duties of Parties	14	17-19	40-41	29-31	29-30	34-35	34-35
19	Termination of Agency	14	19	40	30	29	36	33
Part Five:	Partnerships							
20	General Nature of Partnerships	29	21	43	34	32	37	37
21	Relation of Partners to Each Other	30	22	44	35	33	39	38
22	Relations of Partners to Third Persons	30	23	44	35	33	38	38
23	Dissolution of Partnerships	30	24	43	36	34	40	37
24	Limited Partnerships	29	21	45	33	31	41	39
Part Six:	Corporations							
25	Character, Formation and Powers	31	25	46-47	37, 39	35, 38	42, 44	40-41
26	Capital Stock and Dividends	32	26, 28	48	38	35	43	43
27	Officers, Directors and Stockholders	33-34	27-28	48-49	38	36-37	45-46	44
28	Foreign Corporations	36	30	46	37	-	42	42
29	Securities Regulation and Accountant's Legal Responsibility	35	29	48	37	35, 37	48	43

* Howell, Allison, Alternate Edition same as first edition except alternate edition has Chapter 47, Wills, Trusts and Estates.

Contents

PART FIVE: 82
PARTNERSHIPS

PART SIX: 100
CORPORATIONS

PART SEVEN: 126
PERSONAL PROPERTY AND BAILMENTS

PART EIGHT: 138
SALES AND PRODUCTS LIABILITY

PART NINE: 166
COMMERCIAL PAPER AND SECURED TRANSACTIONS

PART TEN: 196
BANKRUPTCY

PART ELEVEN: 212
REAL PROPERTY AND MORTGAGES

PART TWELVE: 228
WILLS, ESTATES, AND TRUSTS

Digest of
BUSINESS
LAW

PART ONE
Law and Government Regulation

Introduction to Law

I. Nature and classifications.

   A. Definition: Principles and rules of conduct which the governing power recognizes, maintains, and enforces.
   B. Public law and private law.
      1. Public law deals with the State, either by itself or in its relations with individuals.
      2. Private law deals with individuals in their relations with each other.
         a. Laws relating to agreements between persons.
         b. Laws relating to rights and duties of individuals in relation to the person and property of others independent of agreements.
   C. Substantive and procedural law.
      1. Substantive law.
         a. Goes to the merits of the case.
         b. Deals with question of whether a legally protected right for which the law provides a remedy has been violated.
      2. Procedural law.
         a. Legal procedure: manner of bringing a matter before the court, conduct of a hearing, appeal, and enforcement of a right.
         b. Laws relating to due process, evidence, and litigation in general.
   D. Statutory and case law.
      1. Statutory law.
         a. Laws enacted and promulgated by legislative bodies.
         b. Begin as bills, become session laws, finally appear in statutes or codes.
      2. Case law results from judicial decisions and:
         a. Either interprets and applies statutory laws or
         b. Pronounces legal principles where no statutory law is applicable (common law).
         c. Appears in reports.
         d. Serves as legal precedent (*stare decisis*).

II. The judicial system.

    A. Typical structure of a judicial system.

        1. Trial courts.

           a. Referred to as lower or inferior courts.

           b. Have original jurisdiction (power to hear and determine controversy in the first instance).

           c. Evidence presented and facts determined by jury or judge.

           d. Law applied to facts by judge.

        2. Appellate courts.

           a. Hear appeals from trial courts.

           b. Proceeding consists of hearing arguments based on record made in trial court.

           c. Decision of trial court may be affirmed, reversed, or reversed and remanded for further proceedings.

           d. Due process embraces right of appeal.

    B. Dual judicial system in United States.

        1. Federal system.

        2. State systems.

    C. The Federal judicial system.

        1. United States district courts (trial courts).

           a. Each state consists of one or more judicial districts, each having a United States district court.

           b. Original jurisdiction: Federal laws; civil actions where the matter in controversy exceeds $10,000 and there is either a federal question or diversity of citizenship (i.e., parties are citizens of different states).

           c. Venue (place of trial): When founded on diversity, action may be brought in judicial district where all plaintiffs reside or all defendants reside or in which claim arose.

           d. A corporation may be sued in the judicial district in which it is incorporated, is licensed to do business, or is doing business.

        2. United States courts of appeal (intermediate appellate courts).

           a. Eleven judicial circuits in United States, e.g., 7th circuit: Illinois, Indiana, and Wisconsin. One court of appeal in each circuit.

           b. Jurisdiction: Appeals from all final decisions of district courts and most administrative agencies.

        3. United States Supreme Court.

           a. Cases in the courts of appeals may be reviewed by writ of certiorari; by appeal, if state statute is held unconstitutional by court of appeals.

    b. Final judgment of highest court of a state may be
        reviewed by writ of certiorari where consti-
        tutionality of United States or state statute is
        drawn into question or by appeal where decision
        was against validity of United States statute or in
        favor of state statute.
  D. State judicial systems.
      1. Trial courts.
          a. Established by legislative acts.
          b. Jurisdiction varies as to types of cases triable in
              court.
          c. Criminal and/or civil jurisdiction.
          d. Justice of the peace courts, district courts, munic-
              ipal courts, county courts, circuit courts, and small
              claims courts.
      2. Intermediate appellate courts.
          a. In some states.
          b. May have some original jurisdiction.
          c. Due process requires only one appeal.
      3. Court of last resort.
          a. Usually, but not always, called supreme court.
          b. Where no intermediate court, appeal is a matter of
              right.

III. Judicial procedure.

  A. Initiating the action.
      1. Service of summons.
          a. Service may be on defendant, on competent mem-
              ber of family or by publication.
          b. Merely states defendant must respond, or judg-
              ment will be taken against him.
      2. Complaint.
          a. Usually served with summons.
          b. States jurisdictional facts, cause of action, and
              demand for relief.
      3. In response to summons, defendant may:
          a. Do nothing: Default judgment results.
          b. Demur: Facts do not state a cause of action.
          c. Answer: Deny allegations, set up grounds of de-
              fense.
          d. Answer and counterclaim.
  B. Preparation for trial.
      1. Adverse examination: Find out how other party will
          testify.
      2. Depositions taken from out-of-state witnesses.
      3. Demand to admit facts.

      4. Physical examinations.
    C. Trial.
      1. Selection of jury.
        a. *Voir dire:* Examination of jurors to determine ability to serve impartially.
        b. Challenges for cause and peremptory challenges.
      2. Opening statement.
      3. Plaintiff's case in chief.
        a. Testimony of witnesses.
        b. Exhibits.
        c. Judicial notice: Matters of common knowledge need not be proved.
        d. Defendant's motion for nonsuit or directed verdict.
      4. Defendant's case in reply.
        a. Procedure same as in plaintiff's case in chief.
        b. Proof offered in support of answer and counterclaim, if there is one.
        c. Plaintiff's motion for directed verdict.
      5. Plaintiff's case in rebuttal; defendant's case in rejoinder.
      6. Arguments to jury (sometimes called summation).
      7. Instructions to jury.
      8. Verdict: Jury resolves issues of fact.
      9. Decision: Judge applies law to facts.
     10. Judgment: Who won and relief granted, if any.
    D. Appeal.
      1. Initiating the appeal.
        a. Notice filed, served on opposite party.
        b. Bond for costs of other party filed.
        c. Application for stay of judgment made.
      2. Record transmitted to appellate court.
        a. Original papers and exhibits.
        b. Transcript of proceedings.
      3. Brief and appendix prepared by opposing parties.
      4. Oral argument.
      5. Decision and entry of judgment.

IV. Government agencies, boards and commissions.

    A. Created by statute or executive order which:
      1. Delegates authority to carry out policy.
      2. Specifies basic procedural rules.
    B. Legislative function. Agencies make:
      1. Procedural rules: Govern agency proceedings.

    2. Interpretative rules: Interpret statute under which agency functions, e.g., IRS rulings.

    3. Legislative rules: Substantive rules which have force of law, e.g., FTC trade regulation rules.

C. Executive function.

    1. Investigate.

    2. Determine most effective enforcement policy.

    3. Institute appropriate legal proceedings.

D. Quasi judicial function (not all agencies).

    1. Hold hearings similar to trials.

      a. Due process required.

      b. No jury.

      c. Administrative law judge presides and makes initial decision.

    2. Appeal to agency officials.

      a. Arguments concerning prior proceedings and whether statute applies.

      b. Final decision made.

    3. Enforcement: Issue cease and desist order; enforce civil penalty (fine) or obtain injunction in court of law.

E. Appeal to courts of appeal (judicial system).

    1. Stay obtained: postpones effect of agency action.

    2. Appeal from some agencies, e.g., FTC, may be to any circuit in which business is transacted.

F. Grounds for setting aside agency order: Denial of due process, insubstantial evidence, or agency action which is arbitrary, capricious or in excess of authority.

G. Doctrine of exhaustion of remedies: One must make timely use of all rights available under agency procedural rules to be entitled to judicial (court) relief.

H. Concept of agency expertise: Courts will not impose their judgment where agency expertise is involved.

I. Judicial process of inclusion and exclusion: It is ultimately for the courts to determine what activities fall within or outside of congressional acts.

2 Crimes and Torts

I. Criminal law: That body of law dealing with acts or omissions (crimes) considered wrongful against society, for which punishment is prescribed by law and imposed in a judicial proceeding brought by the state.

II. Classification of crimes.

   A. Treason: Levying war against the United States or adhering to its enemies, giving them aid and comfort.
   B. Felony: Any crime punishable by death or incarceration in a penitentiary. The more serious crimes such as murder, rape, arson, and grand larceny are felonies.
   C. Misdemeanor: Any crime punishable by a fine or confinement in a local jail. Consists generally of the lesser offenses such as traffic violations, breach of the peace, or petty larceny.

III. Nature of crimes.

   A. Crimes *mala in se:* Offenses that are wrong in themselves; that is, inherently vicious and bad, such as murder, mayhem, and robbery.
   B. Crimes *mala prohibita:* Offenses that are not morally wrong, but are declared wrongful by the state, such as violations of the traffic laws, antitrust laws, or income tax laws.

IV. Elements of a crime.

   A. A wrongful or overt act, and
   B. Criminal intent (sometimes called *mens rea* or guilty mind).
      1. The accused is presumed to intend the natural and probable consequences of his acts.
      2. The accused is presumed innocent until proven guilty beyond a reasonable doubt.
      3. Minors are capable of criminal intent except that:

a. A child under the age of seven years is incapable of criminal intent.
b. It must be proven that a child between seven and fourteen knew right from wrong.
c. These rules have been changed by statute in some states.

V. Defendant's defenses and rights.

A. An alibi: Proof that defendant was at another place at the time of the crime.
B. Insanity: An insane person is incapable of forming the criminal intent necessary for the crime. Various tests have been used for insanity.
    1. The right and wrong test: The accused who does not differentiate right from wrong is insane.
    2. Irresistible impulse test: The accused whose mental condition was such that he or she possessed an irresistible impulse to commit the crime is insane.
    3. The Durham rule: Accused does not have criminal intent if the crime was a result of mental disease or defect.
C. Entrapment: Where the authorities induce the accused to commit the crime, the criminal intent originated with the authorities, not the accused; therefore there is no liability.
D. Self-defense: Where the accused acted with reasonable cause to protect person or property, then the criminal act is justified.
E. Prohibition against illegal search and seizure.
    1. Must have a search warrant based on probable cause or a search incident to an arrest which is within the scope of the arrest.
    2. Illegally obtained evidence is not admissible at the trial.
F. Miranda warning: Accused must be advised of his right to remain silent and his right to legal counsel before questioning by the authorities.
G. Accused cannot be forced to testify against himself.
H. Double jeopardy: Accused cannot be prosecuted more than once for the same crime. The defendant has the right to appeal the judgment, but the state does not.

VI. Punishments.

A. Death.
B. Imprisonment.
C. Fine.

    D. Removal from office.

    E. Disqualification to hold and enjoy any office or vote.

VII. Law of torts: That body of law dealing with acts or omissions considered wrongful against a person or the person's property, other than a breach of contract, for which a civil action may be maintained for the injury sustained.

VIII. Classification of torts.

    A. Intentional torts against the person or his or her property.

    B. Negligent torts against the person or his or her property.

    C. Strict liability in tort.

IX. Elements of a tort.

    A. Existence of a duty, other than contract, owing by one person to another.

    B. Breach or violation of the duty by the wrongdoer.

    C. Resulting injury or damage to the holder of the right.

X. Intentional torts.

    A. Torts against the person.
        1. Assault and battery: Assault is the threat of putting another person in physical danger. Battery is the actual contact with another person, causing injury.
        2. False imprisonment: Detention of another person against his or her will without probable cause.
        3. Defamation: A publication tending to cause one to lose the esteem of the community. Truth is a complete defense to this tort.
            a. Slander: Oral defamation.
            b. Libel: Written defamation.
        4. Invasion of the right of privacy: Public disclosure of private facts that cause mental anguish to the injured party.

    B. Torts against property.
        1. Trespass to property: Any interference with real or personal property in the possession of another without consent is trespass.
        2. Conversion: An unauthorized exercise of the right of ownership of personal property belonging to another.
        3. Deceit (fraud): Injury resulting from a misrepresentation of a material fact, knowingly made with intent to deceive, which is justifiably relied on by the injured party. (See also Contracts, Chapter 5, Genuineness of Assent.)

C. Remedies.
  1. Actual damages.
  2. In the case of malicious intentional torts, punitive damages may also be awarded by the court.

XI. Negligent torts.

A. Injuries caused by conduct of the wrongdoer which was contrary to the standard of care owed to the injured party and which was the proximate cause of the injury.

B. Standard of care: The degree of care which a reasonable and prudent person would exercise under the same or similar circumstances.

C. Proximate cause: The injury must be the natural and probable consequence of the wrongful act or the injury must have been foreseeable by a reasonable and prudent person.

D. Defenses.
  1. Assumption of risk: Injured party who, by agreement, expressed or implied from the circumstances, enters into a relationship which involves obvious and known danger, has assumed the risk, absolving the wrongdoer from liability.
  2. Contributory negligence: Injured party whose own negligence contributed to the proximate cause of the injury cannot recover.
     a. Last clear chance: Where injured party was initially negligent, exposing himself or herself to harm, but now is helpless to avoid the harm, and the wrongdoer has a last clear chance to avoid the harm but does not, the injured party's negligence is not a defense.
     b. Comparative negligence: Some jurisdictions do not allow contributory negligence as a defense. These jurisdictions allow recovery if injured party is less than 50 percent negligent.

E. Burden of proof.
  1. The injured party normally has the burden of proving the wrongdoer was negligent. Often difficult to prove.
  2. *Res ipsa loquitur* (the thing speaks for itself) shifts the burden of proof to the wrongdoer. If the injured party can show:
     a. The event that injured him or her would not ordinarily occur without negligence, and
     b. The wrongdoer was in exclusive control of the instrumentalities causing the injury, then the wrongdoer must prove he or she was not negligent; otherwise the suit will be lost.

XII. Strict liability in tort.

A. When one undertakes an extremely hazardous activity and injury is foreseeable even in the absence of negligence, the wrongdoer is liable in any event. Examples are blasting activities with powerful explosives and keeping of wild or vicious animals. (See also Chapter 29, Warranties and Product Liability.)

B. Negligence per se (negligence in itself). Where conduct is in violation of a statute enacted to protect persons against certain injuries, injured party need not prove negligence.

Antitrust Laws 3

I.   In general.

   A. Purpose: To preserve the freedom to compete.
   B. Regulation pertains to interstate commerce.
   C. Exemption provided for labor unions.

II. Restraint of trade.

   A. Sherman Act, Section 1: Contracts, combinations, and conspiracies in restraint of trade are illegal.
      1. Rule of reason: Where restraint is insignificant or only in an attenuated sense, it is not prohibited.
      2. Per se unreasonableness: Where restraint has pernicious effect on competition and lacks redeeming virtue, it is conclusively presumed to be unreasonable.
   B. Price fixing.
      1. Price fixing agreements and combinations formed for the purpose and with the effect of raising, depressing, fixing, pegging, or stabilizing the price of a commodity are illegal per se.
      2. Aim: To eliminate price competition, control market.
      3. Fact that price is reasonable or that price competition has had a disastrous effect is no defense.
      4. Exchange of price information may be treated as restraint of trade.
   C. Territorial restraints.
      1. Horizontal arrangements.
         a. Agreement between competitors at the same level of the market structure to allocate territories.
         b. Per se violation of Sherman Act.
         c. Fact that arrangement was developed to increase competition is no defense.
      2. Vertical arrangements.
         a. One manufacturer restricting the territory of his distributors or dealers.
         b. Not illegal.
   D. Refusals to deal.
      1. Individual refusals.

11

        a.   Manufacturer may lawfully refuse to sell to retailer who does not adhere to manufacturer's specified resale prices.

        b.   Manufacturer may not entwine wholesalers in a resale price maintenance plan.

   2. Concerted refusals (group boycotts).

        a.   A horizontal combination of buyers or sellers agreeing not to deal with a certain firm or only with those on a select list.

        b.   Illegal per se if purpose is to stifle competition.

III.   Monopolies.

   A. Sherman Act, Section 2: Monopolizing or attempting to monopolize any part of interstate trade or commerce is illegal.

   B. Monopoly power.

     1. Power to control prices or exclude competition.

     2. Court must decide what constitutes relevant market.

        a.   Cross-elasticity test used: Interchangeability of commodities for same purposes. Reasonable approach.

        b.   Responsiveness of sale of one product to price changes of other considered.

        c.   Establishes "part of commerce" alleged to be monopolized.

     3. However, manufacturer's power over price and production of his own nonstandardized product is not illegal monopoly.

   C. Where combination and conspiracy is proved, scope of market is not in issue.

IV.   Price discrimination.

   A. Clayton Act, Section 2, as amended by Robinson-Patman Act: Unlawful for person engaged in interstate commerce to discriminate in price between different purchasers of commodities of like grade and quality where effect may be to:

     1. Substantially lessen competition or

     2. Tend to create a monopoly or

     3. Injure, destroy, or prevent competition with any person who grants or knowingly receives the benefit of such discrimination, or with customers of either of them.

   B. Commodities of like grade and quality.

1. Have identical physical or chemical characteristics.
2. Identical product cannot be marketed under a private label for less than own brand.

C. Primary level injuries.
   1. Injuries affecting competitors of discriminatory seller.
   2. Usually discrimination between customers in different geographic areas.
   3. Predatory price cutting is illegal per se.

D. Secondary level injuries.
   1. Injuries affecting competitors of favored purchaser.
   2. Quantity or functional discounts resulting in discriminatory price.

E. Tertiary level injuries.
   1. Injuries affecting competitors of the customer of a favored purchaser.
   2. Typically occur where seller uses dual distribution system in same geographical area.
   3. Favored wholesaler passes price differentials to retailers.
   4. Fourth level injuries may also occur which violate law.

F. Statutory defenses.
   1. Cost justification defense.
      a. Sales to a particular buyer result in lower costs relative to other buyers of same class.
      b. Defense turns on acceptability of accounting methods.
   2. Changing conditions defense.
      a. Conditions affecting the market for or the marketability of the goods concerned.
      b. Includes actual or imminent deterioration of perishable goods, obsolescence of seasonal goods, distress sales under court process, sales in good faith in discontinuance of business in the goods concerned.
   3. Meeting competition defense.
      a. Seller may rebut *prima facie* case by showing lower price to purchaser to meet lower price of competitor.
      b. Price met must be a legal one.

G. Indirect price discrimination.
   1. Unlawful to pay or receive commissions, brokerage allowances, discounts, or other compensation except for services rendered.
   2. Unlawful to pay customer for services or facilities unless such payment is available to all competing cus-

tomers on proportionally equal terms.

    3.   Unlawful to furnish one purchaser services or facilities not accorded to all on a proportionally equal basis.

V.   Tying contracts.

    A.   Clayton Act, Section 3: Unlawful to lease or make a sale of goods or fix a price on the condition that the lessee or purchaser shall not use or deal in the goods of a competitor where the effect may be to:
        1.   Substantially lessen competition or
        2.   Tend to create a monopoly in any line of commerce.
    B.   Characteristics of an illegal tying contract.
        1.   Agreement to sell product (tying item) but only if buyer also purchases a different product (tied item).
        2.   Seller has economic power over tying item: holds patent or otherwise dominates market.
        3.   Tied item is readily available in the open market.
        4.   Aim: Eliminate competition in the tied item.
    C.   Defenses.
        1.   Arrangement necessary to maintain product's integrity or to protect goodwill interest in trade name.
        2.   Impractical to separate products.

VI.   Mergers and acquisitions.

    A.   Clayton Act, Section 7: Unlawful for a corporation engaged in interstate commerce to acquire the stock and /or assets of another corporation where, in any line of commerce in any section of the country, the effect would be to:
        1.   Substantially lessen competition.
        2.   Tend to create a monopoly.
    B.   Forms of corporate combinations.
        1.   Merger: Title to all assets of two or more corporations vested in one of them.
        2.   Consolidation: Title to all assets of two or more corporations vested in a newly created corporation.
        3.   Parent and subsidiary: One corporation acquires controlling interest in another.
    C.   Economic characterizations of mergers.
        1.   Horizontal mergers: Merged companies perform similar functions in the production or sale of similar goods.
        2.   Vertical mergers: Merged companies in supplier-customer relationship.

3. Conglomerate mergers.
D. Probable effect of merger established.
    1. Relevant facts concerning the competitive pattern of the industry.
    2. Market affected must be substantial.
        a. Product market (line of commerce) determined by cross-elasticity test.
        b. Geographic market (section of the country) may be national or local.
E. Failing company defense.
    1. Clear probability of business failure.
    2. Efforts to get someone else to buy it have failed.

VII. Interlocking directorates.

A. Refers to persons serving on the boards of directors of two or more corporations.
B. Clayton Act, Section 8, makes interlocking directorates illegal where:
    1. Corporations are engaged in interstate commerce.
    2. Net worth of one is more than $1,000,000.
    3. Elimination of competition by agreements between them would violate antitrust laws.

VIII. Unfair and deceptive acts and practices.

A. Federal Trade Commission Act, Section 5: Unfair methods of competition in commerce and unfair or deceptive acts or practices in commerce are declared unlawful.
B. Unfair acts and practices.
    1. Bait and switch.
        a. Advertising item with no intention to sell.
        b. Switch to a more expensive item.
    2. Shipment of unordered goods.
        a. Follow-up collection letters.
        b. Practice also violates postal laws.
    3. Scare tactics: Misrepresenting dangers in the use of products customer already has or in products of competitors.
    4. Relay salesmanship: Use of more than one sales talk in a single day.
    5. Consistently breaching contracts with customers.
        a. Failure to deliver goods or undue delay in delivery.
        b. Failure to deliver brand advertised.
    6. Causing employees to be disloyal or to tend to misrepresent.

      a.   Lavish entertainment and gifts.

      b.   Secret rebates, payola, and push money.

C.   Deceptive acts and practices.

   1.   Misrepresenting merits of goods.

      a.   Health-giving properties.

      b.   Curative effects.

      c.   Beautifying effects.

      d.   Character, composition, or quality of the goods.

   2.   Puffing (reasonable exaggeration) is not treated as deception.

   3.   Deceptive pricing.

      a.   Claim of saving should be from the usual and customary retail price in the recent regular course of business.

      b.   Preticketing by manufacturer unlawful unless retailers usually sell item at preticketed price.

   4.   Deceptive guarantees.

      a.   Guarantee must clearly and conspicuously disclose at time of sale nature and extent of guarantee, manner in which guarantor will perform, and identity of guarantor.

      b.   Pro rata adjustment of guarantees: Basis on which adjustment will be made must be disclosed at time of sale.

D.   Enforcement.

   1.   Commission has authority to make rules specifying acts or practices as unfair or deceptive.

   2.   Knowingly violating rules or final cease and desist orders covering similar act or practice subjects violator to a fine.

   3.   Commission can seek relief for consumers.

IX.   Antitrust law sanctions.

A.   Criminal.

   1.   Violation of Sherman Act is a felony.

   2.   Corporations fined up to $1,000,000; individuals, up to $100,000 and/or up to 3 years in prison.

   3.   Property transported interstate forfeited if it is subject of a Sherman Act, Section 1, violation.

B.   Civil.

   1.   Violation of any antitrust law: Treble damages, costs and reasonable attorney fees awarded.

   2.   United States limited to actual damages and costs.

C.   Other.

   1.   Violations restrained by injunction.

   2.   Divestiture ordered for unlawful mergers.

PART TWO
Contracts

Introduction 4

I.   A contract is a promise or set of promises, expressed or implied, creating a legal obligation.

II. Elements.

   A. Agreement: Either an expressed offer on the part of one party accepted by another or conduct on the part of two or more parties implying an intent to effect legal contractual relations. Sometimes referred to as manifestation of mutual assent.
   B. Consideration: One generally may not claim a contractual right against another unless a duty was assumed in connection with the promise of the other.
   C. Competent parties: Persons not under "legal disability," adults having sufficient mental capacity to bind themselves to legal obligations.
   D. Legal object: A contractual subject matter which is not against the public interest as such interest is determined by legislative bodies and by the courts.

III. Classification of contracts: Origin.

   A. Express: Arise from either spoken or written words of parties showing an intention to be bound.
   B. Implied: Arise largely from the conduct of the parties from which a reasonable inference can be drawn that the parties intended to bind themselves. Note, also, that provisions may be implied to fill in details of an express contract.
   C. Quasi: Obligations imposed by law without the consent of the parties where unjust enrichment would otherwise result.

IV. Classification of contracts: Nature of undertaking.

   A. Unilateral: A promise for an act. *or an act for a promise. e.g. reward*
   B. Bilateral: A promise for a promise.

19

V. Classification of contracts: Form.

A. Formal.
1. Sealed.
    a. Most common form has word SEAL imprinted after signatures of parties.
    b. Seal defined as anything parties intend to be a seal.
    c. Significance: Solemnity; in some states, presumption of consideration, longer statute of limitations for breach of contract actions.
    d. No significance where UCC applies.
2. Record: Court judgments; debtor-creditor status results.
B. Informal: Simple contract. May be written or oral. Includes all contracts not sealed or of record.

VI. Classification of contracts: Interrelationship of provisions.

A. Whole or entire: A contract in which each term is so closely related to every other term that no part of the contract may be separated from any other part without destroying the basic purposes of the parties.
B. Divisible or severable: A contract in which one or more parts may be deleted without destroying the basic bargain of the parties.
C. Distinction of particular importance in cases involving issue of legality of object or Statute of Frauds.

VII. Classification of contracts: Extent performed.

A. Executed: One completely performed by all parties.
B. Executory: Promises have been exchanged, but performance has not yet occurred.
C. Note: Contracts may be executed on one side but executory on the other; one side may be partially executed and partially executory.

VIII. Classification of contracts: Legal effect.

A. Valid: One that has all of the essential elements of a contract.
B. Void: Lacks one or more contract essentials and has no legal effect. In reality is therefore not a contract.
C. Voidable: Binds one of the parties positively, but other party has option of enforcing or not.

D. Unenforceable: Recourse to the courts is unavailable for enforcement, usually for one of the following reasons:
    1. Rules of procedural law making evidence inadmissible.
    2. Lack of credible witnesses. Enforcement of oral contract depends on credibility of party alleging its existence.
    3. Bankruptcy, laches, and the statute of limitations raising a bar to enforcement.

5 Agreement

I. Agreement results from an offer and an acceptance conforming with and responsive to it.

    A. Sometimes referred to as a meeting of the minds or manifestation of mutual assent.

    B. Means a concurrence of intents, not necessarily simultaneously.

II. Offer.

    A. A proposal made with an intention to be bound contractually. An intention is implied on the part of the party making the proposal, the offeror, that all of the ramifications of an enforceable contractual agreement shall arise from a mere assent to the proposal by the offeree. The following do not come within the meaning of the word *offer* in its legal context:

        1. Invitations to deal (solicitations for offers), i.e., advertisements, price tags and lists, catalogues, circular letters, generalized statements of desires to sell made orally and in writing. However, if proposal may be construed as contemplating acceptance by an identifiable offeree, it is held to be an offer, as in the case of a reward.

        2. Proposals made in jest—test: Would a reasonable person have a right to assume a serious intent on the part of the proposer? The law imputes intention according to the reasonable meaning of words.

        3. Proposals to make a gift: No intention to be contractually bound.

    B. Essentials.

        1. Must be definite and certain. Exception: Contracts for the sale of goods may be made in any manner sufficient to show agreement, including conduct by both parties which recognizes the existence of such a contract. Alternative offers are not treated as indefinite and uncertain.

2. Must contain sufficient terms such that a mere assent will afford a court a basis tor enforcement. Exception: Contracts for the sale of goods do not fail even though one or more terms are left open if there was an intention to make a contract and there is a reasonably certain basis for giving an appropriate remedy.
3. Must be made with intent to create legal relations. Intent is determined by what offeror leads offeree to believe is intended, not by what offeror subjectively intends.
4. Must be communicated from offeror to offeree.

C. Duration. An offer stands open until:

1. Lapse.
   a. A time specified in the offer.
   b. After a reasonable time when no time has been specified.
   c. Death or insanity of offeror or offeree in interim between offer and acceptance.
   d. Destruction of subject matter in interim between offer and acceptance.
   e. Governmental action prior to acceptance making purpose of intended contract illegal.
   f. In contracts for the sale of goods, when there is an order or offer to buy for prompt or current shipment and there is neither prompt shipment nor prompt notification of the acceptance, an offeror may treat the offer to buy as having lapsed.

2. Rejection (by offeree).
   a. A rejection extinguishes an offer when received by offeror. If subsequent acceptance by offeree reaches offeror before rejection, contract is formed and rejection is not effective.
   b. Counteroffers have same legal effect as rejections, unless it is clear that the original offer is still under consideration.
   c. Mere inquiries are not counteroffers.

3. Revocation (by offeror).
   a. May be revoked at any time before acceptance.
   b. Even if a definite time limit is set in an offer, it still may be revoked before that time unless offeree has given something of value to have it held open (option contract). Exception: In negotiations for the sale of goods, an offer by a merchant to buy or sell in a signed writing cannot be revoked during the period the writing states the offer is to be open (but period cannot exceed three months.)

        c.   Revocation of an offer takes effect when communicated to the offeree.

        d.   In an offer for a unilateral contract, offer may be revoked at any time before substantial performance of act called for by offer provided the revocation is in good faith and not to perpetrate fraud by withdrawing the offer arbitrarily to defeat payment.

    4.   Acceptance: Offer merges into contract.

III.   Acceptance.

   A.   By expressed assent.

      1.   An acceptance must be absolute and in accord with the terms of the offer.

      2.   Acceptance which varies from offer more than a mere inquiry becomes a counteroffer and hence a rejection. Exception: In contracts for the sale of goods, a purported acceptance which adds minor terms is not a rejection but an acceptance. The additional terms are to be construed as proposals for addition to the contract. As between merchants, such additional terms become part of the contract unless the offer expressly limits acceptance to the terms of the offer, or the additional terms materially alter the offer, or the offeror notifies the offeree within a reasonable time of any objection to such additions.

   B.   By performance.

      1.   In a unilateral contract, acceptance is substantial performance of the act called for. An offeror who withdraws an offer after partial performance is liable in quasi contract for the benefits received prior to withdrawal.

      2.   An offer to buy goods for prompt or current shipment may be treated as unilateral and be accepted by shipment. Shipment of nonconforming goods is acceptance and, at the same time, breach of contract unless seller notifies the buyer that the shipment is offered only as an accommodation to the buyer.

   C.   By silence.

      1.   Silence alone is not treated as acceptance. However, where there is a duty to speak arising out of a prior course of dealing, where the offer was solicited or invited and/or the interests of justice otherwise require, it will be so held. Reasoning is that contract relations cannot be imposed on others.

2. United States postal regulations make the mailing of merchandise without prior expressed request or consent of recipient an unfair practice, treat the merchandise as a gift, and do not obligate recipient to respond.

D. Acceptance can be only by the person to whom the offer was made. An offer is not assignable.

IV. "Complete when posted" doctrine.

A. Where offeree uses the same medium of communication for transmission of the acceptance as the offeror used for transmission of the offer, the acceptance becomes effective when it is out of the control of offeree on way to offeror.

1. Acceptance of offer, when "complete when posted" rule applies, destroys power of rejection, even if rejection is received by offeror before acceptance is received.

2. Power of revocation by offeror is terminated moment acceptance is beyond control of offeree.

3. However, rejection of offer by mail or telegram does not destroy power of acceptance until received by offeror. In such cases "complete when posted" doctrine is modified in that, to be effective, acceptance must be received by offeror before rejection is received.

4. Communication must be properly addressed and stamped for doctrine to apply.

B. Offeror may prevent the doctrine from being applied by specifying in the offer that he or she is not liable until actual receipt of acceptance.

C. Where offer stipulates a particular mode of communicating acceptance and offeree uses a different mode, acceptance is not complete until received.

D. In the case of a sale of goods, any mode of communication reasonable under the circumstances is sufficient for doctrine to be applied.

6 Genuineness of Assent

I. Contract must be free of factors that result in an agreement which neither party intended or to which one of the parties assented either because of being furnished misinformation or of being prevented by the other from exercising a free and voluntary judgment.

II. Mistake.

  A. Mutual or bilateral.
    1. Identity or existence of subject matter.
    2. Unaware of material facts pertaining to:
      a. Physical condition of subject matter or
      b. Scope of commitment (as where specifications furnished are erroneous).
    3. Remedy of rescission available to either party except where parties consciously assumed risk of mistake.
  B. Unilateral.
    1. Seller unaware of valuable characteristics of subject matter of sale.
    2. Buyer misjudges own needs, ability to pay, and similar personal and extraneous matters.
    3. No relief except where the mistake is not due to negligence, the error is apparent to a reasonable person, and the contract is executory.

III. Misrepresentation.

  A. Fraud: Intentional misrepresentation of a material fact justifiably relied upon by the other contracting party to his or her damage.
    1. Intentional misrepresentation includes:
      a. Originated false statements.
      b. Confirming false impressions.
      c. Half-truths.
      d. Nondisclosure of a material fact.
      e. Failure to reveal defects.
      f. Physical concealment.

2. A fact is material if it goes to the basis of the bargain or if, without it, the contract would not have been made.
3. Fact includes:
   a. The actual state of things.
   b. Expert opinion.
   c. Predictions of future conduct of third persons, where their plans are formulated.
   d. Excludes "puffing," "salesmen's talk," "glamour language," and generalized statements of personal opinion.
4. Reliance is generally presumed except:
   a. Where the misrepresentation involves a matter concerning which truth is apparent.
   b. Where the correct information is readily available.
   c. Where the representation concerns the state of the law.
5. The remedies for fraud are either rescission or compensatory (actual) damages. With either remedy exemplary damages may be awarded.

B. Innocent misrepresentation.
   1. Characteristics same as above except for element of intent.
   2. Remedy of rescission available to injured party, but no right to damages.

IV. Duress.

A. Coercion by means of physical force or unlawful threats to persons or property.
   1. Threat of civil suit not duress, if well founded.
   2. Threat of criminal prosecution is duress.
B. Whether or not duress has occurred in a given case is determined by weighing the nature of the threats against the resisting power of the victim, as determined by education, training, character, age, state of health, and status in life. The same threat might be duress in one case but not in another. Subjective standard.
C. The offended party has the option of rescinding the contract.

V. Undue influence.

A. Contractual assent induced by unfair persuasion of one party by another, as where:
   1. A party is dominated by another or
   2. The relationship between the parties is such that one

of them is justified in assuming that the other will not act in a manner inconsistent with his or her welfare.

B. The allegation of undue influence most frequently occurs where there is a preexisting fiduciary relationship, that is, a relationship of trust, such as guardian and ward, trustee and beneficiary, principal and agent, husband and wife, parent and child, attorney and client, physician and patient, and pastor and parishioner.

C. The offended party has the option of rescinding the contract.

Consideration 7

I. Consideration is essential to the enforceability of executory promises.

II. The nature of consideration.

A. A legal detriment to the promisee with respect to the promise made to that person.
B. Legal detriment is the giving up of a legal right.
C. May consist of either:
1. Promising to do or doing that which the promisee is not legally bound to do or
2. Promising not to do or refraining from doing that which the promisee has a legal right to do.
D. Must be in response to promisor's promise.
E. Need not be of actual benefit to promisor.

III. Adequacy of consideration.

A. Courts generally will not weigh the bargain of the parties but may do so if bargain is unconscionable or specific performance is demanded.
B. Disproportionate consideration may be evidence of lack of reality of consent.

IV. "Already bound" doctrine.

A. Doing or refraining from doing that which one is already bound to do is not a legal detriment and does not constitute consideration.
B. Money obligations.
1. Promising to take or taking less than is due is not supported by consideration where debt is undisputed (liquidated).
2. If debtor takes on an additional obligation, e.g., pays debt before it is due, there is consideration for a reduction of a liquidated debt.
3. Composition agreements.

        a. Purpose: To enable distressed debtor to solve financial problems without going into bankruptcy.

        b. Creditors mutually agree to take less than is due.

        c. Mutual reductions by creditors of amounts owed them are treated as consideration.

    4. Settlement of a disputed (unliquidated) debt for less than the amount claimed is supported by consideration. Note: Cashing or retention of check given "in full payment" is treated as agreeing to settlement (accord and satisfaction).

V. Past consideration.

    A. Subsequent promises for benefits previously received are not supported by consideration.

    B. Exceptions:

        1. New promises to pay in writing where obligations are barred by statute of limitations.

        2. Warranties made after sale of goods.

        3. Where justice requires, courts may treat the past consideration as "moral consideration," supporting the subsequent executory promise.

VI. Illusory promises.

    A. Where no obligation is in reality assumed or promise is indefinite and uncertain, promise is illusory and does not constitute consideration for another's promise.

    B. If right to cancel before performance is absolute, promise is illusory; if right to cancel is conditional, promise is not illusory.

    C. If obligation depends only on what is wanted or desired, promise is illusory; if based on existing needs or requirements, it is not illusory.

VII. Output, requirements, and exclusive dealing agreements.

    A. An offer to buy the output of the seller or to furnish the requirements of the buyer, if made in good faith, will not fail for lack of definiteness and mutuality of obligation, unless unreasonable.

    B. An agreement either by the seller or buyer for exclusive dealing in a certain kind of merchandise creates an obligation by the seller to use best efforts to supply the goods and by the buyer to use best efforts to promote their sale.

VIII. Special situations.

    A. Subscriptions to charitable, religious, and educational enterprises.

        1. Public policy favors enforcement.

        2. Various legal theories are used by courts to sustain subscription.

    B. Sealed contracts.

        1. State statutes provide that seal creates rebuttable presumption of consideration.

        2. Seals are inoperative in contracts for the sale of goods.

    C. Commercial paper.

        1. Rebuttable presumption of consideration as between immediate parties.

        2. Lack or failure of consideration no defense against holder in due course.

    D. Claims arising out of breach of contract can be discharged without consideration by written waiver.

IX. Promissory estoppel. *RED OWL*

    A. In a proper case, justice may require that promise be enforceable without consideration.

    B. Conditions for enforceability:

        1. Promise was one which promisor should reasonably have expected to induce action or forbearance.

        2. Promise did induce such action or forbearance.

        3. Injustice can only be avoided by enforcement of promise.

    C. Only reliance damages are recoverable; i.e., damages may not exceed loss caused by change of position in reliance on promise.

8 Capacity of Parties

I. Minors (infants): At common law, a person under age of
    twenty-one years; by statute in majority of states, under age of
    eighteen years.

    A. Minor's right to disaffirm contracts.
        1. Both executory and executed contracts are voidable,
            not void, at option of minor.
        2. Other party (adult) is bound until minor elects to dis-
            affirm.
        3. Right is absolute and personal only to the minor.
    B. What constitutes disaffirmance (avoidance).
        1. Expressly by written or spoken words.
        2. Impliedly by a course of conduct.
        3. Must disaffirm in total.
    C. Time for avoidance.
        1. Any time during minority or reasonable time after
            reaching majority.
        2. Reasonable time depends on nature of subject matter
            and surrounding circumstances.
        3. Where minor has conveyed real property by deed:
            a. Can retake beneficial use of real property upon dis-
                affirmance during minority but
            b. Cannot set aside transfer of title until majority.
    D. Recovery of property by minor upon avoidance.
        1. Other party must return to minor all consideration re-
            ceived or money equivalent.
        2. Sale of goods: If buyer has transferred goods to good
            faith purchaser for value, minor seller cannot recover
            such goods.
        3. Sale of property other than goods: Minor seller can re-
            cover real property even from good faith purchaser
            from buyer.
    E. Restitution by minor upon avoidance.
        1. By general rule, minor must return whatever consid-
            eration he or she received to extent capable of re-
            turning.

2. Right to disaffirm not affected by fact minor is unable to return the consideration or consideration returned is in damaged condition.

3. By minority rule, must return consideration or money equivalent as a condition of avoidance.

F. Minor's fraudulent misrepresentation of age.

1. No effect on right of avoidance if action is brought against minor on executory contract.

2. If minor seeks to rescind contract, misrepresentation will bar recovery unless minor can restore any consideration received.

3. In some states minor may be liable in tort for damages.

4. Above rules modified by statute in some states.

5. Contracts induced by fraud of any kind, including misrepresentation of age, allows innocent party to disaffirm.

G. Ratification (approval).

1. After ratification, right to disaffirm is lost.

2. Ratification ineffective unless made after minor reaches majority.

3. How made.

   a. Expressly by written or spoken words.

   b. Impliedly by a course of conduct.

H. Contracts for necessaries.

1. Minor liable in quasi contract for necessaries.

   a. Liable for reasonable value, not contract price of necessaries.

   b. Not liable on executory contracts, only necessaries actually furnished and used.

2. Necessaries include only those goods and services which are essential to minor's person in the light of his or her station in life. Subjective standard.

   a. General rule excludes goods and services applicable to minor's property or business.

   b. Minority rule includes business goods and services needed to support self and family.

   c. Not necessaries if parent or guardian ready, willing, and able to provide them.

I. Statutory modifications in various states—educational loans, court-approved contracts, bank accounts, stock transfers, business contracts, and others.

J. Parent's liability for minor's contracts.

1. Generally no liability.

2. Liable for reasonable value of necessaries furnished by third persons where parent had legal obligation to furnish and failed to do so.

3. Any adult who cosigns contract with minor is liable on contract even though minor disaffirms contract.

K. Minor's torts.
1. Liable for torts after reaching the age of reason.
2. But if tort involves the breach of a duty flowing from contract, most courts hold minor not liable.
3. If tort is connected with but independent of contractual duty, minor is liable for tort.

II. Other persons lacking full capacity.

A. Insane persons.
1. One unable to comprehend the subject of the contract, its nature, and probable consequences.
2. Where previously adjudged insane and has a general guardian, contracts are void.
3. Where not previously adjudged insane, contracts are voidable, but, if other party did not know person was insane and contract is fair and reasonable, insane person must return consideration or money equivalent to disaffirm.
4. Insane person's voidable contracts can be ratified or disaffirmed by the person when sane, by a guardian while insane, or by personal representative of the estate after death.
5. Insane persons are liable for necessaries on same basis as minors.

B. Intoxicated persons.
1. Under contract law, a person so intoxicated as not to appreciate his or her acts or consequences thereof is temporarily insane.
2. Above rules pertaining to insane persons apply.

C. Married women.
1. Under common law, married women had no contractual capacity, and their contracts were void.
2. In most states, women have been accorded by statute full capacity and responsibility.

D. Aliens.
1. In peacetime, aliens have substantially same contractual capacity as citizens.
2. In wartime, enemy aliens may not resort to our courts, but if sued, may enter and defend.

E. Corporations.
1. Authority and capacity to contract is governed by charter.
2. Will be fully discussed in chapter on corporations under *ultra vires* acts.

Legality of 9
Object

I. Freedom of contract.

    A. A fundamental right. Public policy favors a broad spectrum of allowable objects or purposes of private contracts.

    B. Competing public policy.

        1. The public policy favoring freedom of private contract gives way when a conflicting public interest is affected.

        2. What constitutes the public interest is determined by legislative bodies in the form of ordinances, statutes, and codes and by the courts in decided cases.

        3. Where the protection of the public interest is deemed necessary, constraints are placed on the freedom of private contract by declaring certain objects or purposes of contracts illegal.

II. Unreasonable restraint of trade.

    A. Where the main purpose is to limit competition, object is against public policy and illegal at common law and under state and federal statutory law. Includes price fixing, dividing the markets, and agreements to limit production.

    B. Where restraint of competition is incidental to a proper main purpose in a contract and is limited in time and area, it may be treated as reasonable and legal.

        1. Employment contracts.

            a. Main purpose is employment. Employee exposed to business secrets, customer lists, and other matters. Employment is of substance.

            b. Employee may agree not to work for a competing employer for a reasonable length of time and within a reasonable area after termination of employment.

            c. Court weighs employer's need of protection against employee's right to work.

        2. Sale of goodwill.

         a. Competition from seller after sale would destroy value of goodwill.

         b. Time and area restraint may not be unreasonable in relation to buyer's need for protection.

III. Usury.

    A. State statutes set maxiumum rate of interest which may be charged. Usury is a loan or forbearance of money at a rate of interest in excess of the statutory maximum.
       1. Court looks through form to substance.
       2. Excessive service charge is treated as interest.
       3. Maximum rates do not apply to purchase money loans, marine loans or loans made to corporate borrowers.

    B. Effect of usury.
       1. Penalities vary widely from state to state.
       2. Range is from limiting lenders' recovery to maximum rate to both forfeiture of principal/interest and criminal penalties.
       3. Lender and borrower not in *pari delicto* (of equal fault); borrower is victim and may benefit.

    C. Time/price differentials.
       1. Refers to a credit price in excess of a cash price in individual sales of goods.
       2. Two prices disclosed (cash price and credit price); customer has option.
       3. Issue of usury not involved but may be regulated by other statutes.
       4. Revolving charge accounts do not involve time/price differentials; result in debtor-creditor relationship; usury laws apply.

    D. Discounting accounts and notes.
       1. Not an initial lending and borrowing.
       2. Accounts and notes are purchased.
       3. Discount rate may yield more than maximum rate. Not within scope of usury law.

    E. Small loan laws.
       1. Need for high risk capital in small loan market.
       2. Finance companies permitted higher maximum rates for "signature loans," etc.
       3. Regulated, usually by state banking commission.

IV. Gambling.

    A. Contracts in which one stands to win or lose something of value dependant upon chance are void by state statutes.

1. Exceptions are made in many states for regulated activities, such as, bingo, pari-mutuel betting, and casinos.
2. Insurance contracts are treated as gambling if insured does not have an insurable interest in the subject matter (property or life insured).
3. Stock and grain market transactions are treated as gambling if intent is not to take delivery but only to settle balances and take profits and losses.

B. Lotteries.
1. Prohibited by state constitutional or statutory law, except in some states where operation by the state is permitted.
2. Elements: Consideration, chance, and prize.
3. Used widely for sales promotions, e.g., sweepstakes and drawings. Legal if one of above elements is not present.
   a. Filling in blank form not treated as consideration.
   b. Entering short essay or poem to be judged not treated as chance.

V. Crimes and torts.

A. Contracts which call for the commission of a crime are void.
B. If crime is incidental, contract may be enforced in some cases.
C. Contracts which call for the commission of a tort are void.
D. Contracts which require the breach of an existing contract are tortious.
1. Contract rights are property rights.
2. Victim has cause of action for damages.

VI. Licensing statutes.

A. Regulatory type.
1. Designed to protect public from unscrupulous and unqualified persons. Provides standards for trades and professions.
2. No recovery on contract where person performing does not have proper license.
B. Revenue type.
1. Merely requires payment of fee for license.
2. Recovery permitted for performance of services even in absence of a license.

VII. Sunday statutes.

    A. In the absence of state statute to the contrary contracts may be entered into and/or performed on Sundays.

    B. Where there are statutory restrictions, Sunday contracts generally may be ratified or adopted on weekdays.

VIII. Effect of illegality.

    A. Contract void if parties are of equal fault (in *pari delicto*). No remedy: court leaves parties where it finds them.

    B. Exceptions:

        1. If a statute, intended to protect members of the public or of a class, makes a contract illegal, a victim may have a remedy under the statute or otherwise benefit, e.g., illegal tying contract, treble damages allowed. (See Chapter 3, Antitrust Law)

        2. If illegal part of contract is executory, party may withdraw and recover money paid or value of goods given.

        3. If one of the parties was justifiably ignorant of facts which make object illegal, action may be maintained against other party for damages.

        4. If contract is divisible, some courts will strike illegal portion and enforce legal part, e.g., union contract with closed shop provision.

        5. "Blue pencil" rule: If covenant not to compete is divisible and consists of reasonable and unreasonable provisions, the latter will be stricken. Trend is toward rule of reasonableness, permitting courts to modify covenant to make it reasonable.

Writing **10**
Requirements

I. Nature of the rule.

   A. If essentials of contract are met, an oral contract is as valid as a written one.

   B. Statutes in all states require certain types of contracts to be in writing.
     1. Known as Statute of Frauds.
     2. If such contracts are oral, then unenforceable.
     3. Statute available only as a defense.
     4. Statute has no effect on fully executed contracts.

II. Types of contracts generally covered.

   A. Contract of the personal representative of a decedent's estate:
     1. To pay debts of the estate out of representative's own funds.
     2. Does not apply to promises to pay estate debts out of estate funds.

   B. Contract to answer for the debt, default, or miscarriage of another person (suretyship).
     1. Must be a secondary or conditional promise.
       a. Must be capable of being reduced to "this is his obligation; if he doesn't perform, I will."
       b. If promise is primary or original, need not be in writing.
     2. Main purpose doctrine.
       a. Main purpose of promise to pay another's debt, if debtor does not pay it, is to serve the pecuniary or business interest of the promisor.
       b. Promise need not be in writing.
     3. A promise made to a debtor to pay the debt is not within the statute.

   C. Contract made in consideration of marriage.
     1. Does not include mutual promises to marry.

2. Does cover contracts where marriage is the consideration for payment of money or transfer of property.

D. Contract involving any interest in real property.
   1. "Any interest" includes life estates, mortgages, easements, and leases for more than one year.
   2. Contract for the sale of goods to be severed from realty. _including gifts_
      a. If minerals, or the like or a structure is to be severed by the buyer, then treated as an interest in real property.
      b. If items above are to be severed by seller, then treated as a sale of personal property (goods).
      c. If timber, growing crops or other things not mentioned in Part a above can be severed without material harm to the realty, then treated as sale of personal property (goods) whether severance is to be by seller or buyer.
   3. Most courts will enforce oral contract for sale of interest in land where buyer with assent of seller:
      a. Makes valuable improvements on the land, or
      b. Takes possession and also pays a portion of the purchase price.
      c. Payment of purchase price alone is not enough.

E. Contract not performable within one year.
   1. If contract by its terms cannot possibly be fully performed within one year, it comes under the statute.
   2. If it can possibly be completed within one year, it is not under the statute.
   3. The one-year period runs from the time contract is made, not from the time performance is to begin.
   4. Oral contract is enforceable where it has been fully performed on one side, even though other side cannot be performed within one year.

F. Contract for the sale of goods.
   1. Applies only if price of goods is $500 or more.
   2. Between merchants, confirming letter not objected to by other party within ten days of receipt satisfies statute.
   3. Not within the statute if:
      a. Goods are specially manufactured for the buyer and not suitable for sale to others, and
      b. Seller has either made a substantial beginning of their manufacture or commitments for their procurement.

4. Oral contract enforceable if defending party admits the existence of a contract in a pleading, in testimony, or otherwise in court, but only as to the quantity of goods admitted.
5. If part payment or partial delivery, then contract is enforceable to extent of part payment or partial delivery but no more.

G. Contract for the sale of securities, regardless of price, subject to exceptions 4 and 5 in Part F above.
H. Contract for the sale of intangible personal property not covered by Parts F and G above if price exceeds $5,000.
I. Many special contracts are required to be in writing by local law.

III. Other provisions of Statute of Frauds.

A. The writing.
1. No particular form required; may consist of one document, or separate papers, letters, etc.
2. Must specify the parties, the subject matter, and any material or special terms.
3. In the sale of goods, it need only indicate contract has been made and state the quantity of goods involved.
4. Must be signed by the party to be charged with performance (defendant).
5. Anything one adopts as a signature stands as such.
6. May be made up after contract is made, but must be in existence at time of trial.

B. If contract involves more than one section of Statute of Frauds, must satisfy both sections.
C. A subsequent mutual rescission or modification of a contract that comes under the Statute of Frauds must also be in writing.
D. Effect of noncompliance.
1. Contract unenforceable, not void.
2. If part performance, recovery in quasi contract to prevent unjust enrichment.

IV. Parol evidence rule.

A. Once the parties have assented to and reduced their contract to a writing, no parol (oral) evidence will be admitted at trial to alter, vary, change, or modify any of the terms of the written agreement.

B. Exceptions to the rule.
   1. Oral testimony to prove contract was void or voidable (fraud, mistake, duress, lack of capacity, illegality, etc.).
   2. Where contract is incomplete, parol evidence admissible to show actual agreement of parties.
   3. Parol evidence to prove entire contract was subject to a condition that prevented the contract from taking effect.
   4. Proof of subsequent oral mutual rescission or modification of the written contract, if contract does not come under Statute of Frauds.
   5. Parol evidence to clarify the terms of an ambiguous contract.
   6. Parol evidence to prove clerical or typographical errors or omissions.
   7. In contracts for the sale of goods, writing can be explained or supplemented by:
      a. Course of dealing or usage of trade or by course of performance.
      b. Evidence of consistent additional terms unless writing intended as a complete and exclusive statement of the agreement.

Rights of 11
Third Parties

I.   A person who is not an original party to a contract is referred to as a third party. Generally, such parties cannot enforce the contract. Exceptions:

    A. Where one qualifies as a third party donee or creditor beneficiary.

    B. Where contract rights have been transferred by assignment.

II. Third party beneficiaries.

    A. Third party donee beneficiaries.

        1. Contract evidences an intent upon the part of a promisee (having privity) that the promisor shall assume a direct obligation to a third person.

        2. Contract may be enforced by third party where it appears that contract was made primarily to confer a direct benefit upon third party.

        3. Third party is not a contracting party, does not have privity, and receives benefit largely as a gift.

        4. Defenses defendant promisor has against promisee are also good against third party.

    B. Third party creditor beneficiaries.

        1. Contract obligates one of the parties to satisfy a duty of the other party to a third person under a preexisting contract.

        2. Third party may enforce contract.

        3. The parties to the contract may vary or rescind the contract at any time:

            a. If the third party does not know of the contract or

            b. If the third party has not changed his or her position in reliance on the contract, or

            c. If the contract is executory on both sides.

    C. Third party incidental beneficiaries.

        1. Persons who will incidentally benefit as a result of the performance of a contract.

        2. Incidental beneficiaries have no right of enforcement.

III.   Assignments.

   A. A transfer of contract rights to a third person without the consent of the contracting party owing the corresponding duty.

      1. There must be a preexisting primary contract from which contract rights are assigned.

      2. Transfer results in a new set of rights and duties called contract of assignment.

   B. Parties.

      1. Obligor: Party who owes the duty which is the subject of the contract of assignment.

      2. Assignor: Party who transfers the right to that duty.

      3. Assignee: Party to whom right is transferred.

   C. Form: May be oral unless primary contract comes within the Statute of Frauds.

   D. Rights which may be assigned.

      1. Nonpersonal rights only may be assigned, i.e., rights to duties which do not involve personal services and rights in which the personal credit or character of the assignor is not a factor.

      2. The right to wages (a nonpersonal right).

         a. With respect to wages, employer and employee stand in debtor-creditor relationship.

         b. May be assigned only where there is existing employment.

         c. Limited in some states by requiring spouse's approval and providing time limit.

      3. Assignment may be prohibited by contract provision to that effect.

         a. In contracts for sale of goods a prohibition of assignment of the contract is to be construed as barring only the delegation of performance unless it clearly bars the assignment of rights.

         b. A right to damages for breach of contract or a right arising out of the assignor's due performance of entire obligation can be assigned despite agreement otherwise.

         c. A prohibition by contract provision of assignments of accounts receivable is ineffective.

   E. Defenses and offsets.

      1. Obligor may set up as a defense or offset any claim against assignee that obligor had against assignor up to the date of notice of the assignment, to the extent of the sum assigned.

2. A buyer's agreement not to assert against an assignee any claim or defense which he or she may have against the seller is enforceable by an assignee, except for sales to consumers in states where the Consumer Act has been adopted and under FTC regulations.
F. Notice.
    1. Obligor is bound to the assignee to the extent of the assignment less any offset, upon receiving notice of the assignment.
    2. The first assignee in point of time prevails over subsequent assignees regardless of order in which assignees gave notice (American rule), except where without knowledge of prior assignment:
        a. Subsequent assignee obtains payment or satisfaction of obligor's duty.
        b. Subsequent assignee obtains judgment against obligor.
        c. Subsequent assignee and obligor enter into a novation (See Chapter 13, Discharge).
    3. In some states, first assignee to give notice has priority (English rule).
G. Implied warranties of assignor.
    1. That assignor will do nothing to defeat or impair the value of the assignment.
    2. That the assigned right is valid and is subject to no defenses other than those apparent at time of assignment.
    3. Does not warrant that the obligor is solvent or will perform obligation.

IV. Delegation of duties.

A. Only nonpersonal duties may be delegated without consent.
B. Original contracting party remains liable for performance.
C. Liability of assignee for performance.
    1. At common law, unless expressly assumed, assignee not liable.
    2. An acceptance by the assignee of an assignment of "the contract" or of "all my rights under the contract" constitutes a promise by the assignee to perform the assignor's duties.

12 Performance

I. Contract provisions.

   A. Variously referred to as terms, clauses, provisions, and covenants.

   B. Independent covenants.
     1. Promises, the duty of and liability for performance of which is unrelated to the obligation of the other party to perform.
     2. Breach does not give other party right to refuse to perform.

   C. Dependent covenants.
     1. Promises, the duty of and liability for performance of which is contingent upon the performance of a related covenant by the other party.
     2. Failure to perform gives other party right to refuse to perform where conditions are involved.

   D. Conditions.
     1. Terms of major importance; go to the heart of the contract; difficult to determine money damages in event of breach; expressed or implied. Failure of performance terminates, abates, or qualifies the principal obligation of the other party.
     2. Kinds of conditions.
       a. Conditions precedent: Require the performance of an act or the occurrence of an event before the other party sustains a duty to perform.
       b. Conditions concurrent: Intended to be performed at relatively the same time.
       c. Conditions subsequent: Require the performance of an act or the occurrence of an event to continue, suspend, release, or abrogate contractual liability on the part of the other party.

   E. Time of performance.
     1. Treated as a condition where it is stated to be "of the essence" or goes to the heart of the agreement.

    2. Where it is a condition, other party not obligated unless time of performance is strictly complied with.

    3. Where it is not a condition, performance within a reasonable time obligates other party, but entitles party to offset for damages.

  F. Satisfaction with performance.

    1. Provision in contract that performance shall be to the satisfaction of other party is a condition of party's liability.

    2. Where personal taste is involved, party to whom performance is due is sole judge as to whether or not he or she is satisfied.

    3. Where personal taste is not involved and performance is measurable by standards, performance which meets the standards satisfies contract requirements.

II. Extent of performance.

  A. Full performance: Performance to the letter of the contract.

  B. Substantial performance.

    1. Substance of agreement performed with some variation from full performance.

    2. Other party may offset damages for variation, if determinable, provided performance was not accepted as is.

  C. Insubstantial performance.

    1. Wide, material, and significant variations from full performance; apparent disregard for contractual duty.

    2. Party insubstantially performing is not permitted to recover unless other party retains benefit which could be returned; liable for damages.

III. Recovery for part performance.

  A. Reasonable value of part performance is recoverable on basis of quasi contract where full performance is excused, as in cases of impossibility.

  B. No recovery in case of willful breach, except where a benefit was conferred which other party fails to return, though capable of doing so.

IV. Breach of contract.

  A. Consists of failure to fully perform any provision in a contract.

  B. Anticipatory breach.

1. Informing another one will not perform or putting it beyond one's power to perform.
2. Treated as ordinary breach even though performance is not yet due.

V. Remedies for breach of contract.

  A. Damages: A determination by a court that an injured party is entitled to a sum of money equivalent to the financial loss suffered by reason of the other party to the contract having failed to fully perform.
    1. General damages: Arise as expected or usual result of breach.
    2. Special damages: Arise from special circumstances known to party failing to perform.
    3. Compensatory (actual) damages: Sum which will compensate injured party, "make him or her whole"; includes both general and special. Requirements:
      a. A breach must have occurred.
      b. Loss must be measurable, not speculative.
      c. Loss must have resulted from the breach.
    4. Liquidated damages: Agreed upon in advance of breach; allowed where damages would otherwise be speculative; not allowed where damages are measurable and amount agreed upon is entirely disproportionate and of a penal character.
    5. Nominal damages: Six cents, awarded when a breach has occurred but amount is not measurable; carries court costs.
    6. Exemplary (punitive) damages: Additional damages awarded when breach has a tortious character as where fraud is involved.
    7. Mitigation of damages: Duty of injured party to minimize damages.
  B. Restitution.
    1. Defaulting party required to return consideration.
    2. Alternative to money damages; employed where justice is better served.
  C. Rescission.
    1. A determination by a court that the contract may be set aside and the injured party relieved of any further duty to perform.
    2. Granted for:
      a. Breach of a condition.
      b. Absence of genuineness of assent.
      c. Lack of contractual capacity.

    D. Specific performance.
        1.   Object of contract is accomplished by the court.
        2.   Granted only when money damages would be inadequate as in the case of sales of real estate, objects of art and stock in closed corporations.
    E. Injunction.
        1.   Equitable remedy: Party is ordered not to breach contract.
        2.   Violation constitutes contempt of court.

VI.   Excuses for nonperformance.

    A. Prevention.
        1.   Party who interferes with other's performance will not be heard to complain concerning other's breach.
        2.   Party prevented from performing may bring action for damages.
    B. Impossibility.
        1.   Supervening impossibility (unanticipated facts to which defaulting party did not contribute) excuses performance:
            a.   Destruction of an irreplaceable subject matter.
            b.   Death or illness in personal service contracts.
            c.   Governmental action making subject matter illegal.
        2.   Unanticipated difficulty does not excuse performance.
            a.   Performance more difficult or expensive than anticipated.
            b.   Loss resulting from such hardships should fall on party who promised to perform.
            c.   Provision should be made in contract for party to be relieved from performance upon the occurrence of strikes and other incidents over which the party has no control.
    C. Commercial frustration.
        1.   Supervening event, totally beyond perception of parties, makes intended purpose of contract unfeasible.
        2.   Elements of frustration defense.
            a.   Principal purposes in making the contract are frustrated.
            b.   Defendant is without fault.
            c.   Occurrence of an event, the nonoccurrence of which was a basic assumption of the contract.

13 Discharge

I. Refers to termination of contractual obligation.

II. Discharge by agreement.

    A. Agreement to rescind.
        1. Parties each give up right to other's performance.
        2. May be implied from conduct of parties.
        3. Right to rescind is limited in cases of contracts made for benefit of third party.

    B. Accord and satisfaction.
        1. New contract (accord) and its performance (satisfaction) substitute for original contract.
        2. When new contract is performed, obligations of parties terminate under both new and old contracts.
        3. Cashing check "in full payment" is accord and satisfaction in cases of unliquidated debts.

    C. Novation.
        1. Parties agree that a new party is to be substituted for an original party.
        2. Remaining party consents to release of withdrawing party who is discharged.
        3. There must be consideration to bind substituted party.
        4. Distinguished from assignment of rights and delegation of duties in that party released has no further obligation, while one who delegates duties continues to be obligated.

III. Discharge by performance.

    A. Contractual obligation is terminated when performance is accomplished, excused (see excuses for nonperformance), waived, or becomes illegal.

    B. Payment as performance.
        1. A check is payment subject to the condition that it clears.
        2. Where debtor owes several sums to creditor, application of payments may be significant with respect to

statute of limitations and creditor's right to security.

    3.   Debtor has right to direct application of payments. If debtor fails so to direct, creditor has right to make application. If neither has done so, court applies in order of maturity and to unsecured obligations first.

C. Waiver of performance.
    1.   Consists of voluntarily giving up a contractual right.
    2.   Purpose: To consummate contract by disposing of minor potential claims.

D. Illegality.
    1.   Distinguished from illegal object in that legal impediment arises subsequent to creation of contract.
    2.   Parties are discharged even though illegality is temporary unless mutually agreed otherwise.

IV.   Bars to the enforcement of contracts.

A. Statute of limitations.
    1.   Limits period of time from the occurrence of a breach within which an action may be brought for a remedy.
    2.   Period varies from state to state. Statutes may provide a longer period for sealed instruments.
    3.   Statute may not be waived by contractual provision.
    4.   Statute applying to debt does not affect creditor's right to security related to debt.
    5.   Statute is tolled (bar removed) by new promise in writing and/or part payment and is extended (time added) by insanity, imprisonment, coverture (marriage) between the parties, and prolonged absences from the state.
    6.   Equitable doctrine of laches is similar to statute of limitations.

B. Bankruptcy.
    1.   Insolvent debtor lists debts in bankruptcy proceeding; creditors are notified and may make claim on assets in bankrupt estate.
    2.   Discharge of bankrupt debtor by court becomes a defense with respect to listed debts.
    3.   Defense may be waived by subsequent promise to pay debt approved by the court.

V.   Discharge by act of other party.

A. Cancellation and surrender.
    1.   Applies particularly to formal contracts—bonds, insurance contracts, leases, and similar documents.
    2.   May be without consideration if consummated.

B. Prevention of performance.
C. Alteration.
    1. Clean hands doctrine: Plaintiff must come with "clean hands," i.e., may not be guilty of wrongdoing with respect to claim.
    2. Plaintiff who has materially altered written agreement without consent of other party cannot recover on it.

PART THREE
Guaranty, Suretyship, and Insurance

Guaranty and Suretyship **14**

I. Guaranty and suretyship in the broad sense mean the same thing.

   A. A contractual relation whereby one person engages to be answerable for the debt or default of another person.

   B. Parties to the contract.
      1. Principal debtor: One directly responsible for performance.
      2. Creditor: One entitled to performance.
      3. Surety: One who assumes liability for principal debtor's performance.

   C. Surety and guarantor distinguished in the narrow sense.
      1. Surety:
         a. Promises to do the same thing as principal debtor undertakes to do.
         b. Obligation created concurrently with that of the principal debtor.
         c. Has primary liability.
         d. Statute of Frauds not applicable.
      2. Guarantor:
         a. Promises to perform only if the principal debtor does not.
         b. Contract of guarantor is separate and distinct from that of the principal debtor.
         c. Has secondary liability.
         d. Statute of Frauds is applicable.

   D. Suretyship and contract of indemnity distinguished.
      1. Surety:
         a. Makes a promise to person who is to receive performance of an act or payment of a debt by another.
         b. Provides security to creditors.
      2. Indemnitor:
         a. Makes a promise to the person who is to perform the act or pay the debt.
         b. Provides security to debtors.

c. Promises to save debtor harmless from any loss incurred from performance of an act or payment of a debt.

E. Interpretation of suretyship contract if ambiguous.

    1. Where surety is guaranteeing payment for future purchases:

        a. In the absence of a time or an amount limitation, the contract is construed as a guaranty for a single purchase rather than a continuing offer.

        b. If there is a time limitation in the guaranty, it is construed as a continuous guaranty for the time stated.

        c. If there is an amount limitation in the guaranty, it is construed as a continuous guaranty with the maximum liability being the amount stated.

        d. If the contract is unilateral, the creditor must notify the guarantor within a reasonable time that credit has been extended.

    2. Ambiguous provisions of surety contracts involving compensated sureties are resolved against the surety.

    3. Ambiguous provisions of surety contracts are construed in favor of uncompensated sureties and against the creditor.

II. Rights of the creditor.

A. May proceed against the principal debtor.

B. May proceed against the surety.

    1. Creditor is not required to give notice of debtor's default unless contract so provides.

    2. If surety contract requires notice of default to surety:

        a. Uncompensated surety will be released if timely notice is not given.

        b. Compensated surety is not released unless delay of notice prejudiced rights.

    3. Creditor can proceed against surety even while holding collateral as security, subject to surety's right of exoneration.

    4. Where surety holds collateral furnished by principal debtor as security, creditor is subrogated to surety's rights in such collateral.

    5. Creditor can proceed against the surety without first proceeding against the principal debtor. Exception: Conditional guaranty such as a guaranty of collection.

        a. Guarantor in a guaranty of collection is not liable unless creditor sues debtor, obtains a judgment,

and the execution of the judgment is returned unsatisfied.

  b. Creditor also required to give notice to guarantor
of default of debtor; otherwise guarantor discharged to the extent of loss due to the lack of
notice.

 6. Liability of cosureties is joint and several.

III. Remedies of the surety.

 A. Right of reimbursement against the principal debtor.
  1. Available only if surety was legally obligated to pay.
  2. Surety can only recover from the principal debtor the
actual amount surety paid.
  3. Surety does not have to pay the debt in full in order to
have right of reimbursement.
  4. Surety cannot pay debt in advance of maturity and demand reimbursement immediately.
  5. Any collateral in the possession of the surety may be
disposed of as far as necessary to satisfy surety's loss.
  6. Statute of limitations runs from time of payment to
creditor.

 B. Right to exoneration.
  1. This remedy is available before surety has performed
obligation.
  2. May go into court and compel the principal debtor to
perform in order to save the surety from a loss.
  3. Available against creditor to the extent of the collateral in the creditor's possession.
  4. Also available against cosureties to the extent of their
liability.

 C. Right to subrogation.
  1. Available only if the surety has fully performed the obligation of the principal debtor.
  2. Surety obtains all of the rights the creditor had against
the debtor, including the right to any security in the
possession of the creditor.
  3. Any surrender by the creditor to the debtor of security
held by the creditor without consent of the surety, releases the surety to the extent of his or her loss of subrogation to that security.
  4. Statute of limitations does not affect rights against collateral held by creditor.

 D. Right to contribution from cosureties.
  1. Where creditor compels one surety to meet the obligation in full, that surety has the right to recover from
cosureties their share of the loss.

2. An extension of time to or a release of one surety releases other cosureties to the extent the released surety would have been obligated to contribute.
3. All cosureties have the right to share in the collateral held by one surety on the same debt.

IV. Defenses of the surety.

A. Defenses available to the principal debtor—such as mutual mistake, fraud, illegality, lack or failure of consideration, undue influence, etc.—are also available to the surety, with three exceptions:
   1. Infancy of principal debtor.
   2. Bankruptcy of principal debtor.
   3. Statute of limitations. Each state has its own statute of limitations.
B. Concealment and nondisclosure by the creditor of material facts affecting the risk, as well as misrepresentation and fraud of the creditor, are defenses personal to the surety. However, misconduct of the principal debtor does not affect the contract between the surety and creditor.
C. Other acts of the creditor which discharge the surety from liability.
   1. Legally binding extension of time of payment.
      a. Releases an uncompensated surety absolutely.
      b. Releases a compensated surety who can show actual injury as a result of the extension agreement.
      c. Does not release surety if extension agreement stipulates reservation of rights against the surety. Such extension binds the creditor only.
   2. Any material alteration in the contract between creditor and principal debtor without consent of the surety discharges the surety.
   3. Release of the principal debtor without consent of the surety discharges the surety unless the release reserves rights against the surety.
   4. Payment of the principal obligation by the debtor or anyone else discharges the surety.
   5. A valid tender of payment made by either the principal debtor or the surety which is rejected by the creditor releases the surety.

Insurance 15

I. Nature of insurance.

  A. Definition.
    1. Single sentence definitions are not adequate. Each case considered on its merits to determine if insurance is involved.
    2. Plan of mutual protection.
    3. Insurance contract: A contract whereby one party agrees to wholly or partially indemnify another for loss or damage which may be suffered from a specified peril.
  B. State regulation.
    1. Statutes.
      a. Prescribe policy content.
      b. Regulate incorporation, licensing, and supervision of insurers.
      c. Regulate licensing and supervision of agents.
    2. Insurance commissioners.
      a. Make rules and regulations enforcing insurance laws.
      b. Have broad, discretionary powers.
      c. Cooperate with National Association of Insurance Commissioners where state regulation has national implications.

II. The contract of insurance.

  A. Contract and policy distinguished.
    1. Contract.
      a. Oral agreement of the parties.
      b. Enforceable as oral contracts in case of fire and auto liability insurance if all essential terms are agreed upon.
      c. Binder: Temporary insurance which applies while insurer is deciding to accept the risk; may be oral or written.

      2. Policy.
         a. Evidence of insurance.
         b. May be reformed to conform to contract in a proper case.
  B. Essential terms.
      1. Subject matter of the contract: Property or life to be insured.
      2. Amount of the indemnity: Policy limits.
      3. Risk or perils to be assumed by insurer.
      4. Term and time when risk is to attach.
      5. Amount of the premium.
  C. Regulation of policy content.
      1. Standard policy or standard provisions and/or specific information to be set forth in policy.
      2. Approval by insurance commissioner and filing of policies.
      3. Style, arrangement, overall appearance, and size of type specified.
      4. Failure to comply: Policy voidable by insured.
  D. Traditional rule of construction: Policy provisions are to be construed most strongly against the company.
      1. Not applied where standard policies or standard provisions are involved.
      2. Individual words construed by the court as a matter of law.
  E. Payment of premium and delivery of policy are not conditions precedent to liability of insurer except in case of life and accident and health insurance where application so provides.

III. Insurable interest.

  A. Relationship between insured and subject matter of insurance.
      1. Occurrence of insured event will cause real loss to insured.
      2. Kinds of losses.
         a. Loss to property.
         b. Liability to others for negligent acts.
         c. Loss of earnings or profits.
         d. Medical expense.
         e. Loss of support and love and affection.
         f. Loss of one's own life.
      3. Absence of insurable interest renders insurance void as gambling contract.

B. Property insurance.
1. Insurable interest is prospect of financial loss. Occurrence of insured event may:
   a. Necessitate outlay of funds to restore property.
   b. Deprive insured of use and benefit of property.
   c. Lessen value of property as security.
   d. Render insured liable to others for decreased value of property.
2. Legal title not essential to validity of insurance. Besides owner, insured may be lessee, mortgagee, or bailee.
3. Insurable interest must be present at time of loss.

C. Life insurance.
1. Unlimited insurable interest in one's own life.
2. Insurance on another's life.
   a. Personal relationship: Members of the family; loss of love and affection satisfies insurable interest requirement.
   b. Business relationship: Insurance on lives of key employees, partners, debtors; recovery only to extent of financial loss.
3. Interest need only be present at inception of policy.

IV. Risk and loss coverage.

A. Fire insurance: Insured protected from loss as a result of destruction or damage to described property as a result of hostile fire.
1. Hostile fire is one which has escaped its confines.
2. Insurer is liable for loss caused directly or proximately by fire. Proximate cause: Unbroken chain of events between cause (fire) and effect (damage): no intervening cause. Fire peril covers proximately caused:
   a. Smoke and water damage.
   b. Theft at time of fire if not excluded by policy.
   c. Explosions caused by hostile fire.
   d. Damage by smoke, water or falling walls caused by fire in adjoining building even though there is no fire damage to insured building.
3. Loss is recoverable though caused by carelessness of insured.
4. Loss not recoverable where caused by willfulness of insured.
   a. Wrongful act of sole stockholder imputed to corporation.
   b. Wrongful act of one joint tenant imputed to other.

5. Location of insured personal property is material to the risk. Change of location without insurer's consent voids policy.

6. If mortgaged property is destroyed and mortgage did not require insurance, the mortgagee has no interest in the proceeds.

   a. Insurance clauses in mortgages and mortgage clauses in policies give mortgagees an interest in proceeds.

   b. Where a policy with mortgage clause is avoided as to mortgagor, mortgagee's right to collect is not affected, unless policy is first rescinded upon notice to mortgagee.

7. Coinsurance: Amount of insurance must be a specified percentage of value of property or insured shares part of loss.

8. Policy cannot be assigned without insurer's consent, since character of person insured is a risk factor.

9. Right to proceeds after loss may be assigned.

B. Automobile insurance.

1. Public liability coverage: Insured protected from loss resulting from claims of third persons for damages arising out of insured's negligent operation of vehicle.

   a. Omnibus clause: Others driving insured vehicle with permission covered.

   b. Direct action and direct liability statutes: Third persons may sue insurer directly; third party beneficiary principle.

   c. Financial responsibility laws: Require production of liability policy or bond for retention of license after accident.

2. Collision coverage: Unintentional damage to insured vehicle by contact with another object.

3. Comprehensive coverage: Almost all risks except public liability and collision.

C. Subrogation.

1. Where insured has a right of action against third party for loss suffered, insurer will succeed to such right of action; i.e., steps into insured's shoes.

2. Does not apply to life or accident and health policies.

D. Life insurance.

1. Types of policies.

   a. Term: Temporary insurance; no loan or cash surrender value.

   b. Straight-life: Payment of premiums required throughout life of insured.

    c.   Paid-up life: Payment of premiums for specified number of years; coverage throughout life of insured.

    d.   Endowment: Insured entitled to payment of face value of policy when it becomes due; payable to beneficiary in the event that insured dies before due date.

2. Payment of premiums.

    a.   Grace period of thirty days usual. Mailing premium during grace period keeps policy in force though not received by company, if check backed by sufficient funds.

    b.   Lapsed policy options: Withdraw accumulated reserve; purchase paid-up policy, term insurance, or extended insurance.

3. Change of beneficiary.

    a.   Unless right to change beneficiaries is reserved, the interest of the beneficiary vests immediately in the policy and the insured cannot name a new beneficiary, borrow on policy, or cash it in without beneficiary's consent.

    b.   If insured is also beneficiary, policy may be sold or assigned even though assignee has no insurable interest in life of insured.

4. Creditors' rights in policies.

    a.   Creditors have no rights in proceeds of policies where there is a designated beneficiary.

    b.   If payable to insured's estate, creditors have same rights as against debtor's other assets.

    c.   Predecease of beneficiary makes policy payable to estate of insured.

    d.   If insured has right to change beneficiary, cash surrender value may become available to creditors through bankruptcy or insolvency, unless prevented by state statute.

    e.   Policy procured by creditor of insured is payable though debt has been reduced below the face of the policy. Some courts hold that the difference is payable to the debtor's estate.

5. Incontestable clause: Provides policy shall not be contestable or avoided after it is in force for a particular period, usually two years. Where age is misrepresented, coverage is adjusted to correct age.

V. Policy defenses.

    A. Representations: Responses of insured to insurer at time contract is in process of formation.
        1. No duty to volunteer information concerning risk.
        2. Misrepresentations make policy voidable by insurer if material and relied upon.

    B. Affirmative warranties.
        1. Representations incorporated into policy.
        2. Common law: If false, insurer may avoid liability whether material or not.
        3. By statute in many states: Insurer may avoid liability if material and relied upon.

    C. Promissory warranties: Conditions subsequent; impose duties on insured; breach constitutes defense for insurer.

    D. Waiver.
        1. Voluntarily giving up known legal right.
        2. May be oral, written (policy endorsement), or implied by law.
        3. Prevents insurer from taking advantage of irregularity or wrong of insured.

    E. Estoppel.
        1. Precludes insurer from alleging or denying a fact in consequence of own previous statement or act of a contrary tenor.
        2. Prevents insurer from misleading insured to believe insurer will not take advantage of a defense that might otherwise be available to him or her.

PART FOUR
Agency

Employment 16

I. Types of relations.

    A. Employer-employee.
        1. Refers to a relation in which one person, employee, works for another, employer, usually under the latter's direction and control on a regular basis.
        2. Relation variously defined by regulatory law and may include servants, agents, and independent contractors.
    B. Master-servant.
        1. Refers to employment relations in which:
            a. Employer has control over manner in which ultimate result is to be accomplished.
            b. Employee does not have power to bind employer on contracts.
        2. Master and servant is traditional legal terminology.
        3. Class includes factory workers, food service employees, and laborers generally.
    C. Independent contractor.
        1. Refers to a relation arising out of a contract for services in which the person for whom service is to be performed:
            a. Has no control over manner in which work is to be done, but only over end result and, consequently,
            b. Is not liable for torts of contractor.
        2. Person performing service may or may not be an employee under regulatory law. Whether he performs his services mainly for one person is frequently a determining factor.
    D. Principal-agent.
        1. Refers to service relations in which one party, agent, has power to bind other, principal, on contracts.
        2. May be employee or independent contractor.

II. Creation of employment relation.

    A. Express or implied contract.
        1. Principles of contract law apply.

67

        a. Consensual relationship.

        b. Must be in writing if cannot be performed within one year.

    2. Implied where one knowingly accepts services.

B. Union contracts.

    1. Set terms of employment.

    2. Union shop provisions: Union membership a condition subsequent to continuing employment.

III. Obligations of employer to employee.

A. Compensation: Reasonable amount if rate not agreed upon, unless:

    1. Intent that services are to be gratuitous.

    2. Services are between members of immediate families (gratuity assumed).

B. Safe place of employment.

    1. State "safe-place statutes" require employer to provide safe place of employment, safety devices, and safeguards as well as safe methods and processes. Violations subject employer to penalty.

    2. Federal standards adopted under Federal Occupational Safety and Health Act of 1970 (OSHA).

C. Indemnification or compensation for personal injuries.

    1. At common law:

        a. Employer not liable unless negligent.

        b. Defenses of employer:

            (1) Fellow servant doctrine.

            (2) Assumption of risk.

            (3) Contributory negligence.

        c. Recovery in form of damages.

        d. Court action necessary.

    2. State and federal employers' liability acts.

        a. Employer not liable unless negligent.

        b. Common law defenses eliminated.

        c. Recovery in form of damages.

        d. Court action necessary.

    3. Workmen's compensation.

        a. Issue of negligence and common law defenses eliminated.

        b. Only issues are:

            (1) Are employer and employee subject to act?

            (2) Was employee injured performing services growing out of or incidental to employment?

            (3) What is extent of injury?

          (4) What amount of compensation should be paid?

    c. Recovery intended as compensation (according to schedule) rather than damages.

    d. Administrative hearing; no jury trial.

IV. Obligations of employee to employer.

    A. Services.
        1. Perform according to terms of employment agreement.
        2. Implied terms:
            a. Honesty and loyalty.
            b. Obey instructions.
            c. Use due care.

    B. Inventions.
        1. Belong to employee unless otherwise agreed.
        2. "Shop right" rule: Employer has nonexclusive license.

    C. Trade secrets.
        1. May not reveal to others.
        2. In court, regarded as a qualified privileged communication.
            a. Employee may not be questioned about trade secret where disclosure would depreciate value unless relevant to issue and necessary.
            b. May be disclosed in judge's chambers.

V. Liability for employee's torts.

    A. Employee liable for own torts.
    B. Employer liable to third persons if tort within scope of employment of servant or agent (doctrine of *respondeat superior*).
        1. May be out of scope of employment even if done:
            a. During working hours.
            b. Within employer's place of business or with employer's equipment.
        2. Employer is not liable for employee's willful or malicious acts having no connection with employment.
        3. Employer may not escape liability simply because employee was overzealous, overenthusiastic, mean, or vicious in execution of authority.
    C. Fact that employee is retained in his employment after tort has occured and employer has knowledge of it constitutes ratification by employer.

VI. Termination of employment relation by employer.

A. Without cause, if employment is at will.
B. Otherwise, only for just cause, i.e., violation of express or implied terms of employment contract.
C. If employer breaches contract, employee has duty to mitigate damages.

The Agency Relation

17

I.   A consensual relation—expressed, implied, or imposed by equity—in which one party, the principal, delegates to another, the agent, the power to bind him or her on contracts with third persons.

II. Creation of agency relation.

  A. By agreement.
    1. Agreement establishes express authority.
    2. In addition to express authority, agent has implied authority to do whatever is usual or necessary to carry out object of agency.
    3. The form of the appointment of an agent by agreement must be of equal dignity to the act to be done.
  B. By ratification.
    1. Principal expressly or impliedly approves an act after it is done, for which authority had not been granted in advance.
    2. Ratification relates back to when act was done and binds principal from that time, provided:
      a. Purported agent intended to have acted for that principal when he did the act,
      b. Third person was unaware of lack of authority,
      c. Principal was in existence and capable of authorizing act when it was performed, and
      d. Principal has full knowledge of surrounding and essential facts at time of ratification.
    3. Third party can withdraw from the contract any time before it is ratified by the principal.
    4. Ratification must be of equal dignity in form to act done and of entire contract.
    5. Where a contract has been entered into by an impersonator, the person being impersonated may ratify the impersonator's act and claim the benefits thereof.
    6. Retention of employee with knowledge of employee's tort is treated as ratification of wrongful act.

C. By estoppel.
1. Principal has not granted authority, but has created a situation which leads third persons to believe, to their detriment, that agency authority has been granted. Apparent or ostensible authority.
2. Principal's words and/or conduct preclude (estop) him or her from denying actual authority in court.
D. By operation of law.
1. Wife becomes agent of husband for purchase of necessities not supplied by him; children become agents of parents for same reason.
2. By statute, use of highway by nonresident deemed appointment of state officer as attorney upon whom legal processes may be served.
E. By necessity. Emergencies may provide authority to obtain medical services for others or protect goods of others from loss.

III. Classification of agents.

A. General agents: Authority to represent principal is coextensive with principal's business in a given locality.
B. Special agents: Authorized to transact only specific business matters.
C. Professional agents.
1. Travel agencies and advertising agencies usually represent customer. In event of agency's failure to remit, customer has no recourse against transportation firm or media and remains liable on contracts made.
2. Real estate brokers usually are agents of seller for sole purpose of soliciting offers.
3. Auctioneers have dual agency. Represent both buyer and seller for purpose of accepting bid.
4. Automobile agencies usually are treated as independent contractors.
D. Attorney in fact (power of attorney).
1. Has power to sign formal documents.
2. Need not be an attorney at law.
3. Appointment must be in writing and under seal.

IV. Authority of agents.

A. Actual authority: Powers granted by principal to agent.
1. Express authority: Powers granted orally or in writing.
2. Implied, incidental, and customary authority.
a. Power not expressly granted but reasonably necessary to carry out express powers.

      b. Express authority stated in terms of objectives or general terms; agent determines actions necessary to implement.

      c. Includes powers usual and customary in similar agency situations.

B. Apparent or ostensible authority.

    1. Power which the agent appears to have by reason of the manner in which the agent (or servant) is held out by the principal to the public.

    2. Based on principle of estoppel: Principal leads third person to believe authority exists; third person changes position and suffers loss.

    3. May result from ratification or failure to disaffirm prior unauthorized acts.

C. Emergency authority.

    1. Principal not available.

    2. Emergency calls for act beyond agent's express authority.

    3. Agent's duty of diligence requires action to protect principal's interests.

D. Secret limitations.

    1. Third party has right to assume agent has usual and customary powers of agents of same class or type.

    2. While unusual limitations communicated to agents by principals are binding on them in regard to duty to obey instructions, they are not binding on third persons unless communicated to them.

E. Apparent limitations.

    1. In general, agents do not have implied or apparent power to borrow or deal in commercial paper on behalf of principals.

    2. An agent does not have the apparent power to sell principal's goods merely because the agent lawfully possesses them.

    3. An agent who has actual and/or apparent authority to sell does not have the apparent power to extend credit. A limitation to sell for cash only is presumed.

    4. An agent who has actual and/or apparent authority to sell on credit or installments does not have the apparent power to make collections after delivery of the goods.

    5. An agent who has authority to find a purchaser ready, willing, and able to buy does not have the apparent power to bind the principal on contract.

    6. Limits on apparent powers are modified where neces-

sary to performance of authorized acts or acts customary to the particular trade or business.

F. Appointment of subagents.

1. An agent may delegate mechanical or ministerial acts to a subagent if not expressly prohibited from doing so by principal and if subdelegation is necessary to carry out express powers.

2. An agent may not delegate to subagent act that involves personal skill, judgment, or trust unless he or she does so with the knowledge and consent of the principal.

3. In emergencies, power to subdelegate is enlarged.

4. Principal has same responsibility with respect to lawfully appointed subagents as with ordinary agents.

G. Agent need not have contractual capacity to exercise his or her powers on behalf of principal.

H. Agency authority is not created by mere existence of a parental or marital relationship but may arise by actual or apparent grant of authority.

V. Proof of agency relation.

A. Burden of proof is on third party except that there is a rebuttable presumption that driver of vehicle is agent of owner.

B. Agency relation can be established only by proof of words or conduct of alleged principal granting or implying actual or apparent authority. Agency cannot be established by words of agent alone.

Rights and Duties of the Parties

18

I. Obligations of the principal to agent.

   A. Employment consistent with agency agreement.
      1. Principal may not make demands on agent which are unreasonable in relation to objectives of agreement.
      2. Principal may not act so as to impede agent in accomplishment of objectives.

   B. Compensation.
      1. Reasonable amount if rate not agreed upon unless intent that services are to be gratuitous has been expressed or may be implied because rendered by a member of the immediate family.
      2. Real estate brokers and commission salesmen.
         a. Entitled to commission when they find a buyer ready, willing, and able to purchase. Principal assumes risk of nonperformance in the absence of agreement to the contrary.
         b. Advances against future commissions generally treated as minimum compensation.

   C. Reimbursement and indemnification.
      1. Liable for reimbursement of expenses in execution of agency objectives provided they were reasonably necessary and not expressly prohibited in advance.
      2. Liable for losses to agent's property incurred in execution of agency through no fault of agent.
      3. Must indemnify or compensate for personal injury as in the case of employees generally.

II. Obligations of agent to principal.

   A. Loyalty.
      1. May not benefit beyond agreed compensation.
         a. All benefits and opportunities accrue to principal.
         b. Agent is mere conduit in principal's relation to third parties.

        c.   Agent liable to principal for benefit received from third person even though principal not damaged.

    2.   May not deal with principal on own account or represent principals with conflicting interests unless all know and consent.

B. Obey instructions.

    1.   Agent is liable to principal for any damage caused by material deviations from lawful instructions.

    2.   Exceptions:

        a.   Emergency and principal unavailable.

        b.   Ambiguous instruction: Capable of more than one interpretation.

C. Diligence.

    1.   Agent must exercise due care in acting for principal, and if due care is not exercised, agent is liable for damage caused.

    2.   Due care is that degree of care which an ordinary prudent person (average careful person) would exercise under the same or similar circumstances.

D. Account.

    1.   Agent must account for all money and goods which come into his or her hands for principal.

    2.   Agent who intermingles principal's funds with own funds or banks principal's funds in own name is responsible for loss of those funds even if not lost by his or her fault.

E. Notice.

    1.   Agent must give principal notice of all important facts coming to his or her attention and relating to the agency.

    2.   Rule is correlative to the rule that notice to the agent is notice to the principal.

III.   Obligations of principal to third persons.

A. Contracts.

    1.   Principal is responsible for all contracts made by agent on his or her behalf if within the scope of the agent's authority.

    2.   Burden of proof is on third party to show agent had either express, implied, apparent, or emergency power.

    3.   Defense that principal had placed limitations on agent's powers which were neither communicated to third party nor apparent is ineffectual.

B. Torts (doctrine of respondeat superior).

    1.   Principal is liable to third persons for torts of agent if

acts were done within scope of agent's employment.
2. Test of whether act is within scope is same as in employment relation generally, i.e., was he or she pursuing employer's interests.

IV. Obligations of third persons to principal: Since agent is mere intermediary, principal has privity of contract with third party and may enforce contract against third party directly.

V. Obligation of agent to third persons.

A. Ordinarily, agent will not have liability to third persons, since he or she is merely acting in a representative capacity.
B. Agent becomes personally liable when he or she:
1. Acts in excess of authority.
a. Agent impliedly warrants authority.
b. Warranty may be expressly or impliedly waived.
2. Acts for nonexistent principal, e.g., purports to represent a pretended corporation.
3. Knows of principal's incapacity and third party's ignorance of it.
4. Collects more than the amount due or amounts previously paid and has not yet remitted to the principal.
5. Commits an illegal act, even though authorized by the principal.
6. Commits a tort.
a. If outside the scope of employment, agent alone is liable.
b. If within the scope of employment, both agent and principal are liable.
7. Has failed to make it clear to third party that he or she is acting in a representative capacity.
a. Failed to disclose principal
b. Signed name as agent without specifying principal and indicating act is in a representative capacity for that principal.

VI. Obligation of third persons to agent.

A. Ordinarily, third person is not liable to agent for breach of contract made on principal's behalf.
B. Agent may sue third party for breach of contract:
1. Where third party did not know of existence and identity of principal.

      2. Where agent is transferee of rights under the contract as:

        a. Assignee or

        b. Agent for collection.

      3. Where agent has lien on goods for advances, commissions, or expenses. May assert lien against third persons.

VII. Undisclosed and partially disclosed principals.

    A. Agent either pretends to be acting on his or her own behalf or reveals only that he or she is acting as an agent without identifying principal.

    B. Principal may reveal himself or herself and enforce contract against third person, unless it is under seal or is in form of a negotiable instrument.

    C. Third person can sue either agent or undisclosed principal but may not have a judgment against both.

    D. Principal will not be liable to third person where:

      1. Contract is under seal and is not for the sale of goods.

      2. Contract is in the form of commercial paper.

      3. Principal has made a complete settlement with the agent before third person knows of principal.

    E. Parol evidence rule does not prevent undisclosed principal from establishing agency.

Termination of Agency

I. Mutual agreement.

II. Expiration of agreement.

    A. Automatically terminates when specified date for termination arrives.

    B. In absence of expiration time provided, may lapse after a reasonable time where agent has been inactive.

    C. Notice to agent not required.

III. Accomplishment of purpose.

    A. Single purpose agency automatically ceases when purpose is accomplished.

    B. Where several nonexclusive agents are engaged, fulfillment of objective by any one ends authority of others.

    C. Notice to agents or third persons not required.

IV. Operation of law.

    A. Termination is effective automatically for the following causes:

        1. Death of either principal or agent.

        2. Adjudicated insanity of either principal or agent. Prior to adjudication, insanity of either may render contract voidable by principal.

        3. Bankruptcy, where it affects the subject matter.

        4. Destruction of the subject matter.

        5. War, where principal and agent live in hostile countries and commercial relations have been suspended or transactions could not be carried out practically.

        6. Dissolution of partnership or corporate principal.

        7. Change of law making objective of agency illegal.

    B. Notice to agents or third persons not required.

V. Termination of authority.

    A. Distinguish power from right to terminate authority.

      1. Except where nonterminable, as described later, parties have power to terminate authority unilaterally at will. May be subject to damages.

      2. Parties have right to terminate authority unilaterally at will only for cause, i.e., material violation of contract duty.

  B. Revocation of authority by principal.

      1. Principal may recall agency authority at will even though doing so violates agency contract (power to terminate authority).

      2. If principal does not have the right to do so, as where agent has not violated contractual duties, he or she may be liable to agent for money damages.

  C. Renunciation of authority by agent.

      1. Agent may renounce agency at will even though doing so violates agency contract (power to terminate authority).

      2. If agent does not have the right to do so, as where principal has not violated contractual duties, he or she may be liable to principal for money damages.

VI. Nonterminable authority.

  A. Authority coupled with an interest.

      1. Agent has an interest in the thing which is the subject matter of the authority, rather than a mere interest in that which is produced by its exercise.

      2. Authority is absolutely nonterminable as long as agent's interest in subject matter continues.

  B. Authority coupled with an obligation.

      1. Agent (lender) has security interest in subject matter of agency as well as authority to sell subject matter in event of default and apply proceeds to loan. Authority nonterminable until loan repaid. Equitable interest.

      2. However, where agent does not have security interest in subject matter, but only right to sell for reimbursement of monies due from principal, agency is terminated by principal's death.

VII. Effect of termination.

  A. Agent's actual authority ceases.

  B. Agent may continue to have apparent authority.

      1. Where agent wrongfully exercises authority, having apparent power, and third party is unaware of termination, principal continues to be liable to third party.

2. To avoid liability on subsequent unauthorized contracts of ex-agent, ex-principal must give notice to
third persons of termination of agency, except where:
   a. Agency terminated by operation of law.
   b. Agent was special agent.
C. Notice of termination.
   1. Actual notice.
      a. Personal notice: Oral or written notice com-
municated directly to third parties.
      b. Required with respect to those who dealt with
agent prior to termination of agent's authority.
      c. Fact that principal was unaware of dealings does
not excuse notice.
   2. Constructive notice.
      a. Notice by publication in a newspaper of general
circulation.
      b. Required with respect to those who did not deal
with agent prior to termination of authority.
      c. Principal's obligation to general public is satisfied
by public notice of change of status.

PART FIVE
Partnerships

General Nature 20
of Partnership

I. A partnership is a voluntary association of two or more persons to carry on a business for profit as co-owners.

   A. Test for determining the existence of a partnership.
      1. Except for partnership by estoppel, persons who are not partners as to each other are not partners as to third persons.
      2. Co-ownership of property does not of itself establish a partnership, whether such co-owners do or do not share any profits made by the use of the property.
      3. The sharing of gross profits does not of itself establish a partnership.
      4. The receipt by a person of a share of the net profits of a business is *prima facie* evidence that he or she is a partner in the business, but no inference of the existence of a partnership relation shall be drawn where the profits are received in payment of:
         a. A debt by installments or otherwise.
         b. Wages of an employee or rent to a landlord.
         c. An annuity to a widow or representative of a deceased partner.
         d. Interest on a loan, though the amount of payment varies with the profits of the business.
         e. Consideration for the sale of the goodwill of a business or other property by installments or otherwise.

II. Partnership property.

   A. All property orginally brought into the partnership stock or subsequently acquired by purchase or otherwise, on account of the partnership, is partnership property.
      1. Unless the contrary intention appears, property acquired with partnership funds is partnership property.
      2. Any estate in real property may be acquired in the partnership name. Title so acquired can be conveyed only in the partnership name.

83

B. Conveyance of partnership real property.
1. If title is in the name of all partners, conveyance by all partners passes good title.
2. If title is in the partnership name:
   a. A conveyance in partnership name by one partner conveys a voidable title unless the partner had actual or apparent authority or there is a subsequent transfer to a bona fide purchaser.
   b. A conveyance in one partner's name transfers equitable title if that partner had actual or apparent authority.
3. If title is in one or more but not all of the partners' names:
   a. A conveyance by partner(s) holding title conveys a voidable title unless the partner(s) had actual or apparent authority or the purchaser is a holder for value without knowledge of partnership's interest.
   b. Any one partner can transfer equitable title if he or she has actual or apparent authority.

III. Property rights of partners.

A. The property rights of a partner are:
1. Rights in specific partnership property.
2. Interest in the partnership.
3. Rights to participate in the management.
B. Partners are co-owners of specific partnership property, holding as *tenants in partnership*.
1. Unless agreed otherwise, each partner has an equal right with the other partners to possess specific partnership property for partnership purposes but no right to possess it for any other purposes without the consent of the other partners.
2. No partner can make an individual assignment of his or her rights in specific partnership property.
3. A partner's right in specific partnership property is not subject to attachment or execution by his or her individual creditors.
4. Partnership property is subject to attachment or execution by partnership creditors, and no partner can claim any right to it under the homestead or exemption laws.
5. On the death of a partner, his or her right in specific partnership property vests in the surviving partners, and upon the death of the last surviving partner, that person's right in such property vests in his or her legal representative.

6. A partner's right to specific partnership property is not subject of dower, curtesy, or allowances to widows, heirs, or next of kin.
C. A partner's interest in the partnership is his or her share of the profits and surplus and is personal property.
D. A partner can assign his or her interest in the partnership, and such assignment will not of itself dissolve the partnership.
   1. The assignee is not entitled to interfere in the management of the business or to require that the books of the firm be made available for his or her inspection.
   2. The assignment merely entitles the assignee to receive in accordance with the contract the profits to which the assigning partner would otherwise be entitled and, in the event of dissolution, to receive the assignor's interest.
E. A partner's interest is subject to a charging order.
   1. A partner's individual judgment creditor can apply to the court for an order charging the interest of the debtor partner with the unsatisfied amount of the judgment debt.
   2. The court may appoint a receiver who will receive the partner's share of the profits and any other money due him or her from the partnership.
   3. The court may also order that the interest charged be sold.
   4. Neither the charging order nor the sale of the interest will cause a dissolution of the partnership.

21 Relation of Partners to Each Other

I. Partners may regulate their rights and duties to each other by the partnership agreement.

   A. In the absence of an agreement the rights and duties are fixed as a matter of law.
   B. The relationship is basically that of principal and agent; consequently the partners have those duties to the partnership and to their copartners as agents ordinarily have to their principals.
   C. Partnership is a fiduciary relationship requiring utmost good faith, undivided and continuous loyalty among the partners.
      1. No personal advantage may be taken of partners' mutual relations.
      2. A partner holds as trustee for the partnership any benefits or profits gained without consent of the other partners from any transaction connected with the partnership, including use of partnership property.

II. Right to participate in management of the firm.

   A. Each partner has an equal voice in the management of the firm, unless otherwise agreed. Participation is not controlled by capital contribution.
   B. Internal matters: In matters pertaining to relations of partners to one another, majority opinion controls, except that unanimous consent is required for:
      1. Reducing or increasing the capital of the partners.
      2. Embarking upon a new business.
      3. Admitting new partners to the firm.
      4. Contravention of any other agreement between the partners.
   C. External matters: In any other business matter, majority opinion controls, except that unanimous consent is required for:
      1. Assigning the firm property to a trustee for the benefit of creditors.

2. Confessing a judgment against the partnership.
3. Submitting a partnership claim or liability to arbitration.
4. Disposing of goodwill or doing any act making continuation of partnership business impossible.

D. Right to information.
1. Each partner is entitled to full and complete information concerning the conduct of the partnership business.
2. Each partner shall at all times have access to and may inspect and copy any part of the partnership books and records.
3. Unless agreed otherwise, the partnership books are kept at the principal place of business of the partnership.

III. Other rights and duties of partners.

A. Profits, losses, and compensation. Unless agreed otherwise:
1. Profits and losses are shared equally, not in proportion to capital contributions.
2. Losses are shared in the same proportions as profits.
3. There is no right to compensation for services except that a surviving partner is entitled to reasonable compensation for winding up the partnership affairs.

B. Interest, reimbursement, and contribution. Unless agreed otherwise:
1. There is no right to interest on capital contributions until after the date it should have been repaid.
2. There is a right to interest on any payment or advance beyond the agreed capital contribution.
3. The partnership must indemnify and reimburse any partner who makes payments or incurs personal liability in carrying out the ordinary and proper business of the partnership.
4. Where a partner's contribution to make up a loss exceeds the proper share of the loss, he or she has the right of contribution from copartners.

C. Right to an accounting.
1. Accounting cannot be obtained at law but is a proceeding in equity, and the courts must be satisfied that it is necessary; generally, they will grant an accounting only in the event of a dissolution.
2. Equity courts may grant an accounting in the following cases, where no dissolution is contemplated:

    a. Where the partnership agreement provides for an accounting in certain instances or at a definite date.

    b. Where one partner has withheld profits from secret transactions involving partnership business.

    c. Where a partner is wrongfully excluded from the partnership business or possession of its property by copartners.

    d. Where an execution has been levied against a partner's interest.

    e. Where a partner is denied access to the books.

    f. Where insolvency is approaching and all partners are not available.

    g. Whenever other circumstances render it just and reasonable.

D. Continuation after expiration of the agreed term.

  1. When a partnership for a fixed term or particular undertaking is continued after the termination of such term or undertaking without any express agreement, the rights and duties of the partners remain the same as they were at such termination, so far as it is consistent with a partnership at will.

  2. A continuation of the business by the partners or such of them as habitually acted therein during the term, without any settlement or liquidation of the partnership affairs, is *prima facie* evidence of a continuation of the partnership.

Relations of Partners to Third Persons

22

I. A partner is an agent of the partnership for the purpose of its business; and the general laws of agency are applicable to his or her conduct.

   A. The act of every partner apparently for carrying on the business of the partnership binds the partnership, unless the partner had in fact no authority and the person with whom he or she is dealing was aware of the lack of authority.

   B. An act of a partner which is not apparently for carrying on the business of the partnership does not bind the partnership unless authorized by the other partners.

II. Implied authority of partners.

   A. Each partner has the implied power to do all acts necessary for carrying on the partnership business.

      1. The nature and scope of the business and what is usual in businesses of the same kind determines the extent of the implied powers.

      2. Partners in a trading partnership have implied authority to borrow money and to deal with commerical paper, while a partner in a nontrading partnership does not.

   B. Limitations and enlargements of implied powers.

      1. By agreement, partners may limit their powers or distribute them among themselves.

      2. Third persons are not affected by such divisions or limitations unless they have knowledge thereof.

      3. Partners may enlarge their implied authority by agreement, ratification, and estoppel.

      4. Power of action requiring unanimous consent can be delegated by unanimous agreement to one or more partners for performance.

III. Partnership by estoppel.

   A. If a person, by words or conduct, represents himself or her-

self or consents to being represented by another to anyone:

   1.   As a partner in an existing partnership or

   2.   As a partner with one or more persons not actually partners, then:

B. He or she is liable to any such person to whom such representation has been made if:

   1.   There is reliance on such representation, and

   2.   Such person gave credit to the actual or apparent partnership.

C. If a person has made or consented to the representation being made in a public manner, then he or she is liable if credit is extended to the actual or apparent partnership, even though the creditor did not know of the representation.

D. If partnership liability results, the apparent partner has same liability as actual partner.

E. If no partnership liability results, the apparent partner is liable jointly with the other persons, if any, who consented to the contract or representation causing liability.

F. If a person not a partner holds himself or herself out to be a partner in an existing partnership and all members of the firm consent to it, a partnership obligation results.

G. If fewer than all members of the firm consent, it is the joint obligation of the person holding himself or herself out to be a partner and those partners consenting to it.

H. The doctrine of partnership by estoppel only imposes liability; it does not in fact create a partnership or make a person an actual partner in an existing partnership.

IV.   Notice to one partner is notice to all.

A. Knowledge must be acquired while acting within the scope of partner's authority on partnership business.

B. Where fraud is being committed against the partnership by or with consent of a partner, such partner's knowledge is not imputed to the other partners.

V.   Extent and nature of partner's liability.

A. Contractual liability is joint, which means:

   1.   Each living joint obligor must be made a party defendant in any lawsuit on the contract.

   2.   The judgment must be against all of the obligors or none.

3. The death of a joint obligor terminates his or her liability.
4. A release of one joint obligor releases all.
B. Tort liability of partners is joint and several.
   1. Joint and several obligors can be sued jointly, or separate actions may be maintained and separate judgments obtained.
   2. A release of one joint and several obligor does not release the others.
C. The partnership incurs tort liability for all wrongful acts or omissions of any partner acting in the ordinary course of the partnership business and for its benefit.
D. Liability of incoming partner.
   1. Incoming partner does not become personally liable for existing partnership debts unless he or she voluntarily assumes them by word or act.
   2. Incoming partner's interest, including agreed capital contribution, is subject to satisfaction of all partnership debts.
   3. Incoming partner is personally liable for all subsequent obligations of the partnership.

23 Dissolution of Partnerships

I. Dissolution defined: Any change in the relation of the partners caused by any partner ceasing to be a member of the partnership for any reason.

A. Dissolution of an existing partnership also occurs when a new partner is admitted.
B. Dissolution can occur without winding up and termination.
C. Termination occurs when, after dissolution, the partnership affairs are wound up and the business is terminated.

II. Partnerships may be dissolved in three ways:

A. By an act of the parties.
   1. Without violation of the partnership agreement.
      a. By termination of a definite term or particular undertaking specified in the agreement.
      b. By the express will of any partner when no definite term or particular undertaking is specified.
      c. By the express will of all the partners who have not assigned their interests or allowed a charging order against their interest.
      d. By expulsion of any partner from the firm in good faith in accordance with such a power given by the partnership agreement.
   2. In violation of the partnership agreement.
      a. Each partner has the power, but not necessarily the right, to withdraw from the partnership.
      b. Wrongdoer is liable for damages.
      c. In computing the wrongdoer's interest in the partnership, no goodwill shall be taken into account.
      d. If the remaining partners continue the business during the agreed term of the partnership, they may use the wrongdoer's capital during such term.
B. By operation of law.

1. Death of any partner.
2. Bankruptcy of any partner or the partnership.
3. Any event that makes it unlawful for the business to continue.

C. By order of the court.
   1. Whenever a partner is judicially declared insane or shown to be of unsound mind.
   2. Whenever a partner becomes incapable of performing his or her part of the partnership agreement.
   3. Whenever a partner is guilty of conduct adversely affecting the business.
   4. Whenever a partner willfully persists in breaking the partnership agreement.
   5. When the business of the partnership can only be carried on at a loss.
   6. Upon application of the purchaser of a partner's interest, if it is a partnership at will or the term of the partnership has run out.
   7. Whenever other circumstances render dissolution equitable.

III. Effect of dissolution.

A. Dissolution terminates the actual authority of any partner to act for the partnership except so far as may be necessary to wind up the partnership affairs.
B. If dissolution is caused by the act, bankruptcy, or death of a partner, each partner is liable to the other partners for his or her share of any liability incurred on behalf of the firm after dissolution, just as if there had been no dissolution, unless:
   1. The dissolution was caused by the act of any partner and the partner incurring the liability had knowledge of the dissolution.
   2. The dissolution was caused by the death or bankruptcy of a partner and the partner incurring the liability had knowledge or notice of the death or bankruptcy.
C. When a partner retires from the firm or dies and the business is continued by the remaining partners, the withdrawing partner is entitled to the value of his or her interest on the date of dissolution, payable to the retired partner or to the deceased partner's estate, as an ordinary creditor of the partnership.
   1. He or she is entitled to interest on the value of the interest from the date of dissolution, or at his or her option,

2. He or she is entitled to the profits attributable to the use of his or her right in the property of the dissolved partnership.
3. His or her rights are subordinate to those of creditors of the dissolved partnership.

IV. Liability to third persons after dissolution.

A. The dissolution of the partnership does not of itself discharge the existing liability of any partner.
B. In order to terminate the apparent authority of partners and to relieve withdrawing partners of subsequently incurred liability after dissolution where the business is continued, notice must be given to third persons.
1. To all who have had credit dealings with the partnership, actual notice is necessary.
2. To all others, public notice by newspaper publication is sufficient.
3. No notice is required where:
   a. The business has become illegal.
   b. The third person is dealing with a bankrupt partner.
   c. The withdrawing partner is unknown and inactive in the partnership affairs, so that third persons are unaware that he or she was a partner (dormant partner).
C. Where the partnership business is continued without winding up and termination, creditors of the old partnership are also creditors of the new partnership.

V. Distributions upon dissolution and winding up.

A. Upon dissolution and winding up the business of a solvent partnership, the assets are distributed in the following order of priority:
1. Amounts owing to creditors other than partners.
2. Amounts owing partners other than for capital and profits.
3. Amounts owing to partners with respect to capital.
4. Amounts owing to partners with respect to profits.
B. If the partnership is insolvent:
1. The partners individually must contribute their respective shares of the losses in order to pay the partnership creditors in full.
2. If any partner for any reason does not contribute his or her share of the losses, the other partners must contrib-

ute the additional amount to pay firm creditors, in the relative proportions in which they share profits and losses.

3. Any partner who has contributed more than his or her proper share of the losses has a right of contribution against the partners who have not contributed their proper share.

C. Where the partnership is insolvent and/or one or more partners are insolvent, the doctrine of marshalling of assets is applied, as follows:

1. Partnership creditors have priority in partnership property.

2. Partners' individual creditors have priority in individual property.

3. Where a partner is insolvent, the claims against his or her separate property rank in the following order:

    a. Amounts owing to separate creditors.

    b. Amounts owing to partnership creditors.

    c. Amounts owing to partners by way of contribution.

24 Limited Partnerships

I. A limited partnership is a partnership formed by two or more persons under statutory authority, having as members one or more general partners and one or more limited partners.

A. General partners have unlimited liability.

B. Limited partners are not personally liable on the obligations of the partnership.

II. In order to form a limited partnership, partners must file a certificate in the county where the partnership has its principal place of business; it must contain the following information:

A. The name of the partnership.

B. The character of the business.

C. The location of the principal place of business.

D. The name and place of residence of each member, general and limited partners being so designated.

E. The term for which the partnership is to exist.

F. The amount of cash and description of and the agreed value of other property contributed by each limited partner.

G. The additional contributions, if any, agreed to be made by each limited partner and the times at which they shall be made.

H. The share of the profits each limited partner shall receive.

I. If the partners agree, the following powers can be granted in the certificate:

1. When the contribution of each limited partner is to be returned.

2. The right of a limited partner to substitute an assignee as contributor in his or her place.

3. The right of the partners to admit additional limited partners.

4. The right of one or more of the limited partners to priority over other limited partners in the return of contributions.

     5. The right of the remaining general partner or partners to continue the business on the death, retirement, or insanity of a general partner.

     6. The right of a limited partner to demand and receive property other than cash in return for his or her contribution.

III.   Name of the limited partnership.

   A. The surname of a limited partner shall not appear in the partnership name, unless:

     1. It is also the surname of a general partner, or

     2. Prior to the time he or she became a limited partner, the business had been carried on under a name in which the limited partner's surname appeared.

   B. A limited partner whose name wrongfully appears in the partnership name is liable as a general partner to partnership creditors extending credit to the partnership without actual knowledge that he or she is not a general partner.

IV.   A limited partner shall not become liable as a general partner unless, in addition to the exercise of rights and powers as a limited partner, he or she takes part in the management and control of the business.

V.   The contribution of a limited partner may be cash or other property but not services.

VI.   The rights, powers, and liabilities of partners.

   A. The rights, powers, and liabilities of a general partner are substantially the same as those of a partner in a general partnership.

   B. A limited partner shall have the same rights as a general partner to:

     1. Inspect and copy any part of the partnership books at any time.

     2. Have on demand true and full disclosure of information concerning the partnership affairs.

     3. Have dissolution and winding up by court order.

     4. Receive his or her contribution and share of the profits at the appropriate time.

   C. A person can be both a general partner and a limited partner at the same time.

   D. A limited partner is liable to the partnership for the difference between the contribution actually made and that stated in the certificate as having been made.

E.   When a return of all or part of the contribution is received, a contributor is nevertheless liable to partnership creditors whose claims arose prior to the return, but not in excess of the amount returned.

VII.   The partnership is not dissolved by the death of a limited partner, by a limited partner's assignment of his or her interest, or by the admission of a new limited partner.

VIII.   Order of priority of distribution upon dissolution.

A.   To creditors of the partnership.
B.   To limited partners in respect to their share of the profits and income on their contribution.
C.   To limited partners in respect to the capital of their contributions.
D.   To general partners other than capital and profits.
E.   To general partners with respect to profits.
F.   To general partners with respect to capital.

PART SIX
Corporations

25

Character, Formation, and Powers

I. Classification of corporations.

    A. Private stock corporations.
        1. Organized under general business corporation statutes.
        2. Bank, insurance, and railroad corporations are organized under separate statutes.

    B. Nonstock corporations are organized under a separate, not-for-profit corporation statute.

    C. Public corporations are created by government to carry on governmental functions. Sometimes called municipal corporations.

    D. Professional corporations. Most states have statutes allowing the practice of professions by duly licensed individuals under corporate form.
        1. The licensed professional is still fully liable for his or her professional acts.
        2. Permitted in order to obtain tax advantages of corporations not allowed to individuals or partnerships.
        3. Name of corporation must be followed by the letters S.C. (Service Corporation) or P.A. (Professional Association).

    E. Domestic versus foreign corporations. A corporation is said to be domestic in the state of its incorporation and is regarded as foreign in every other jurisdiction.

II. A corporation is an artificial, intangible being created by law.

    A. A corporation is a resident for purposes of taxation and court jurisdiction.

    B. A corporation as a person.
        1. A corporation is a person under the Fifth and Fourteenth Amendments of the United States Constitution, which provide that no "person" shall be deprived of "life, liberty, or property without due process of law."
        2. A corporation is a person under the Fourteenth Amendment, which provides that no state shall "deny to any

person within its jurisdiction the equal protection of the laws."

3. A corporation is not a person under the Fifth Amendment, which provides a "person" the privilege against compulsory self-incrimination.

4. A corporation is not a person under statutes licensing "persons" to practice a profession.

C. A corporation is not a citizen under the Fourteenth Amendment, which provides that "no state shall make or enforce any law which shall abridge the privileges or immunities of citizens of the United States." Therefore, the states have the power to regulate foreign corporations (See Chapter 28).

D. A corporation as a legal entity.

1. A corporation is a legal entity entirely separate and apart from its shareholders, with rights and liabilities entirely distinct from theirs.

2. Piercing the corporate veil. The corporate entity will be disregarded by the courts whenever it is used to defeat public convenience, justify wrong, protect fraud, promote crime, or circumvent the law. In such instances, the shareholders are held accountable.

III. Formation of the corporation.

A. Authority for formation.

1. State legislation provides blanket authority for formation.

2. General incorporation acts specify routine procedure to be followed.

B. Procedure.

1. Execution of the articles of incorporation.

2. Filing the articles of incorporation with the secretary of state.

3. Certified copy of the articles of incorporation is recorded in the office of the register of deeds.

4. Register of deeds notifies secretary of state of the recording.

5. Certificate of incorporation or charter is issued by the secretary of state. In most states, corporate existence commences at this point.

6. Meeting of incorporators is held to organize and adopt by-laws and elect directors.

C. The corporate name.

1. The corporate name must include "corporation,"

"company," "incorporated," or "limited" or end with an abbreviation of one of them.

2. A corporate name cannot be the same as or deceptively similar to the name of any domestic corporation or that of a foreign corporation authorized to do business in the state of incorporation.

3. Usually a corporate name can be reserved for a limited period before incorporation.

IV. Existence of the corporation.

A. A de jure corporation is a corporation which has fully complied with the requirements of the law and whose existence cannot be challenged by anyone.

B. A de facto corporation is a corporation which operates as a matter of fact but has no existence as a matter of law.

1. Its right to exist can be attacked generally only by the state.

2. To have a de facto corporation free from collateral attack it is necessary that:

a. There be a valid law under which the corporation could be and was attempted to be organized;

b. That the law has been substantially and in good faith attempted to be complied with; and

c. That there has been a user of the corporation in carrying on business.

C. Defective incorporation.

1. Most jurisdictions hold that members of a business association, which is neither a de jure nor a de facto corporation, have unlimited liability upon its contracts whenever the association is permitted by the members to be held out as a corporation, on the theory that any association which is not a corporation is a partnership.

2. Some jurisdictions hold that members of defective corporations who are not active in management do not have liability to third persons, but that actions may be maintained against:

a. Agents of the association for breach of implied warranty of authority, or

b. Agents and those members who acted as their principals as joint venturers.

3. Statutes in some states impose unlimited liability upon officers and, in others, upon stockholders for failure to comply with a variety of corporate statutory

requirements pertaining to organization, publicity, and failure to file reports.

    4. It has also been held that continuing to do business after the charter has expired will make participating stockholders liable as partners.

V. Subscription contracts.

  A. Subscription and purchase distinguished.

    1. Subscriber has the rights of a stockholder from the moment of subscription. Therefore, if the corporation subsequently becomes bankrupt, the subscriber is still obligated to pay in the unpaid subscription.

    2. Purchaser does not have rights of a stockholder until stock certificate is issued to him or her. Therefore, if the corporation subsequently becomes bankrupt, the purchaser is not obligated to pay in the unpaid purchase price since the corporation is no longer able to issue the stock certificate.

    3. A subscriber can enforce specific performance of his or her contract, while a purchaser is entitled to damages for breach of contract.

  B. Subscriptions prior to incorporation.

    1. Most jurisdictions hold that a subscription is an offer to become a stockholder and can be revoked before acceptance.

    2. Some jurisdictions hold that a subscription contract between subscribers, when a mutual undertaking, is a mutually binding contract.

    3. Many state statutes provide that subscription contracts are irrevocable for a period of six months.

  C. Subscriptions after incorporation.

    1. Subscription treated as contract of sale when corporation accepts offer. Purchaser must pay for stock to have stockholder rights.

    2. Some states treat contract same as subscription.

  D. Payment by subscribers.

    1. Par value shares cannot be issued for less than par, that is, at a discount.

    2. Neither promissory notes nor promises of future services constitute payment for shares.

    3. Corporation cannot commence business until minimum capital has been paid in.

      a. Minimum capital amount varies from state to state.

      b. If the corporation commences business before

minimum paid in, the directors are personally liable up to that amount.

   c. Some states do not have this rule.

VI. Promoters are persons who prepare the incorporation papers, procure subscriptions, and enter into contracts in anticipation of the creation of the corporation.

   A. Promoters' contracts.

     1. Preincorporation contracts not binding on the corporation, even though entered into in the corporate name.

       a. May be expressly or impliedly adopted by the corporation after it comes into existence.

       b. Statutes in some states impose liability on the corporation.

     2. Promoters are personally liable on these contracts, even though adopted by the corporation.

   B. Fiduciary duty of promoter.

     1. Must make full disclosure in all transactions with subscribers and the corporation.

     2. Must account to the corporation for any secret profits.

VII. Bylaws.

   A. Bylaws are the permanent rules for the conduct of internal corporate affairs. Generally not of public record.

   B. They are binding upon stockholders and officers but not upon third persons who have no knowledge of them.

   C. Usually deal with:

     1. Issue and transfer of stock.

     2. Time, place, and notice of stockholders' meetings.

     3. Powers of and limitations upon the board of directors in the management of the corporation.

     4. Appointment of officers and their powers, duties, and compensation.

     5. Handling of funds and declaration of dividends.

     6. Amendment of bylaws: power vested in board of directors unless reserved to the shareholders by the articles of incorporation.

VIII. Corporate powers.

   A. Express powers are those enumerated in the articles of incorporation and the enabling statute under which the corporation is organized.

   B. Incidental powers are those recognized by courts as being essential to effect the operation and conduct of corporate affairs arising from the legal entity concept of a corporation; they are usually contained in the enabling statutes and include the following:

1. The power to exist perpetually, establish bylaws, make rules and regulations for its management, and have a seal.
2. The power to make contracts, acquire and transfer property, borrow money, execute commercial paper, and sue and be sued in the corporate name.
3. All other powers which are necessary to carry out the corporation's express powers.

IX. *Ultra vires* acts.

A. A corporation has authority only to act within the limitations of its charter and statutory powers. Any acts outside this authority are *ultra vires,* therefore unenforceable.
B. At common law, either party to a contract could use *ultra vires* as a defense.
C. Statutes in most states abolish the defense of *ultra vires,* except that *ultra vires* can be the basis for:
    1. Injunction proceeding brought by a shareholder against the corporation.
    2. Representative suit by the corporation against the officers or directors for engaging in *ultra vires* acts.
    3. Proceeding by the attorney general of the state of incorporation to dissolve the corporation for engaging in *ultra vires* acts.

X. Consolidation and merger.

A. Corporation does not have implied power to sell or lease all of its assets, merge, or consolidate.
    1. Requires approval of at least a majority of its outstanding stock.
    2. Dissenting stockholder entitled to fair market value of stock exclusive of appreciation in anticipation of merger. Stockholder:
        a. Must file a written objection prior to or at the special meeting called for approval.
        b. Must vote against approval or abstain from voting.
        c. Must file written demand for payment of the fair market value of the stock within ten days of the special meeting. Valuation is the fair market value of the stock on the day preceding the special meeting.

B. Merger is the combination of all the assets of two or more corporations, title to which is vested in one of them, known as the surviving corporation.

C. Consolidation is the combination of all the assets of two or more corporations, title to which is taken by a newly created corporation known as the consolidated corporation.

D. Parent and subsidiary corporation: The acquisition by one corporation, the parent, of the controlling interest of another, the subsidiary. No statutory procedure required as there is in the case of a merger or consolidation.

E. Purchase or lease of all assets of another corporation requires consent of shareholders of selling corporation only.

26

Capital Stock and Dividends

I. Shares of stock owned by a shareholder are intangible and invisible things; a right to participate.

    A. Right is evidenced by a stock certificate.

        1. It is a quasi-negotiable document.

        2. A transferee becomes the owner of the shares upon proper negotiation but is not recognized as a shareholder by the corporation until his or her name is registered on the corporate stock book.

    B. Classes of shares.

        1. Common stock: Represents residual ownership and predominant voice in management.

        2. Preferred stock: Stock with special contractual relationship with corporation.

            a. Contract is made up of the stock certificate, articles of incorporation, and the general incorporation statutes.

            b. Contract rights cannot be changed unless the right to do so was reserved when contract was made.

        3. Par value and no par value stock.

            a. Par value stock: Stock issued with a designated face value.

            b. No par value stock: Stock issued without a designated face value.

    C. Watered stock.

        1. Exists when stock is issued in exchange for overvalued property or issued at a discount.

        2. Subsequent creditors of the corporation can sue the shareholders for the amount of the "water."

        3. In the absence of fraud in the transaction, the judgment of the board of directors or the shareholders, as the case may be, as to the value of the consideration received for shares shall be conclusive.

    D. Treasury stock.

        1. By weight of authority, a corporation may acquire its own stock for a legitimate purpose, provided:

        a. Creditors are not injured as a result of a substantial decrease in the equity cushion.

        b. The transaction is not made for the purpose of manipulating control of the corporation.

        c. Acquisition conforms with conditions imposed by statute.

    2. Many states require that such purchases be made only to the extent of unrestricted retained earnings and that the corporation be solvent both before and after the purchase.

    3. All jurisdictions recognize a corporation's right to acquire its own stock: ·

        a. As a gift.

        b. In compromise of a dispute or to prevent a loss.

        c. For purpose of eliminating fractional shares.

    4. Treasury stock cannot be voted, no dividends of any kind are payable upon it, and no preemptive rights of shareholders exist with respect to it.

II. Transfer of shares.

    A. Method is by indorsement and delivery of the certificate. Certificate is then delivered to corporation for transfer on corporate books.

    B. Right to transfer is absolute unless prevented by statute. It may be required to be in conformity with charter or bylaw restrictions.

        1. Any restrictions on transfer must be noted conspicuously on the stock certificate.

        2. As long as restriction on transfer is reasonable, it will be upheld.

    C. Transfer is controlled by Article 8, Investment Securities, of the Uniform Commercial Code.

    D. Forged or unauthorized signature on issue of stock renders the certificate invalid, except that the unauthorized signature of the president or other employee of the issuer or of the registrar or transfer agent is effective in favor of a bona fide purchaser for value and without notice of the lack of authority of the party signing the certificate.

    E. Forged or unauthorized indorsement.

        1. Indorser warrants that there are no forgeries.

        2. No one can take good title through a forgery.

        3. However, a bona fide purchaser is fully protected if issuer reissues or registers the transfer.

    F. Overissue.

        1. Issuer must purchase shares in the open market, or

2. Pay person entitled to issue on the basis of the last sale.
G. Lost, destroyed, or stolen certificates.
  1. Request replacement within reasonable time.
  2. File indemnity bond.
  3. Satisfy other reasonable requirements.
H. Attachment of stock: Can be made only by the actual seizure of the outstanding certificate by the officer making the attachment or levy.

III. Dividends.

A. Types.
  1. Cash dividends.
  2. Stock dividends.
    a. A proportional distribution of additional shares of the capital stock of the corporation.
    b. Merely a capitalization of surplus.
    c. Psychological dividend in that no asset of the corporation is distributed.
    d. Not the same as a stock split, where each share is split into two or more shares by lowering the par or stated value.
B. Sources of cash dividends.
  1. Varies from state to state as follows:
    a. Only out of accumulated earnings.
    b. Only out of excess of assets over liabilities, including capital stock.
    c. Only if corporation is solvent both before and after the dividend.
  2. Sources under the Model Business Corporation Act, which has been followed by many states:
    a. Corporation may not be insolvent.
    b. Only out of unrestricted earned surplus, except that dividends can be paid out of capital surplus if:
      (1) Corporation is solvent.
      (2) Authorized by articles of incorporation or majority of shareholders.
      (3) All preferential dividends have been paid.
      (4) Sufficient net assets remain to cover liquidation preferences.
      (5) Identified and disclosed to the recipients as a dividend from capital surplus.
    c. Can also pay dividends out of capital surplus to discharge cumulative dividend rights if there is no

earned surplus, the corporation is solvent, and full disclosure is made.

3. Nimble dividends: Some states allow dividends out of current earnings even though there is no earned surplus.

4. Dividends on preferred stock.
   a. Generally held to be cumulative unless specifically stated to be noncumulative.
   b. If noncumulative, dividend not payable unless declared. (Minority rule—payable to extent earned.)

5. Dividends not a debt of the corporation until declared.
   a. Once declared, cash dividend declaration cannot be revoked unless dividend was illegal.
   b. Stock dividends can be revoked unless actually distributed.

C. Illegal dividends.

1. Directors liable for illegally declared dividends.

2. Stockholders also liable for illegal dividends received if they knew dividends were illegal.

3. Even innocent stockholders must return illegal dividends if corporation is insolvent.

4. If illegal dividends declared but not yet paid, stockholders or creditors can obtain court injunction against payment.

27 Officers, Directors, and Stockholders

I. Directors are selected by the shareholders collectively to conduct corporate affairs.

  A. Powers are limited by statute, articles of incorporation, and bylaws.
  B. Collective action is required as a group.
    1. Directors cannot vote by proxy.
    2. A majority of the directors constitutes a quorum unless a greater number is required by the articles of incorporation or bylaws.
    3. A majority of the directors present at a meeting at which a quorum is present can transact any business.
    4. Unless prohibited by the articles of incorporation or the bylaws, the directors can take action by unanimous written consent without a meeting.
  C. Directors are elected at the annual meeting of the shareholders to hold office for one year or until their successors are elected and qualify.
    1. Directors may be removed for cause by action of the shareholders.
    2. One or more of the directors can be removed with or without cause at a special meeting of the shareholders called for that purpose.
    3. A vacancy on the board may be filled by the affirmative vote of a majority of the remaining directors.
  D. The board of directors shall consist of one or more members as fixed by the articles of incorporation or the bylaws.

II. Liability of directors.

  A. Directors who vote for or assent to the following acts are jointly and severally liable to the corporation:
    1. Illegal dividends.
    2. Illegal purchase of treasury shares.
    3. Distribution of assets upon liquidation before all creditors are paid.

    4.   A loan to an officer or director, unless authorized by the shareholders.

    5.   Carrying on business before the minimum capital has been paid in.

    6.   Losses incurred by engaging in *ultra vires* activities.

B.   A director present at a meeting is presumed to have assented to all action taken unless:

    1.   His or her dissent is entered in the minutes of the meeting, or

    2.   Written dissent is filed with the secretary during or immediately after the meeting.

    3.   The right to enter or file a dissent does not apply to a director who voted in favor of such action.

C.   A director is not liable under 1, 2, or 3 of Part A above if he or she relied in good faith upon financial statements represented to be correct by the president or officer in charge of the books, or statements prepared by a CPA or in good faith considered the assets to be of their book value in determining the amount available for dividends or other distribution.

D.   Directors also have civil and criminal liability for negligence and mismanagement of the corporation.

III.   Officers.

A.   The officers are elected by the board of directors and can be removed by the board.

B.   The corporation must have at least a president, one or more vice presidents, a secretary, and a treasurer.

C.   Any two or more offices may be held by the same person, except the offices of president and secretary cannot both be held by the same person at the same time.

D.   All officers and agents of the corporation have such authority in the management of the corporation as may be provided in the bylaws or as may be determined by resolution of the board of directors not inconsistent with the bylaws.

E.   Officers have civil and criminal liability for negligence and mismanagement of the corporation.

IV.   Fiduciary duties of officers and directors to the corporation and its shareholders.

A.   Loyalty and good faith are required of officers and directors.

    1.   Must fully disclose any possible interest in corporate transactions.

2. Cannot make a secret profit by the use of inside information which is available by reason of position (corporate opportunity).

B. Contracts between directors and the corporation and between corporations having common directors.
   1. Voidable if contract is not honest and fair.
   2. Require full disclosure of all the facts and circumstances.
   3. Burden is upon interested directors to show their fairness.
   4. If the interested director's presence is necessary for a quorum, or if his or her vote is necessary in order to pass a resolution regarding the transaction, the action is voidable at the election of the corporation.

C. Purchases and sales of stock by officers and directors.
   1. Majority rule: Officer or director has no fiduciary duty to shareholder as long as he or she did not make any fraudulent misrepresentation about the stock.
   2. Minority rule: Officer or director has fiduciary duty to shareholder to make full disclosure at least of special circumstances he or she has knowledge of because of position in the corporation.
   3. Today the trend is toward the minority rule.
   4. SEC disclosure requirements and six months rule: Each officer and director and each beneficial owner of more than 10 percent of the registered equity securities of a corporation must disclose dealings in such securities and is liable to the corporation for any profit made on purchases and sales of them within the six-month period. (See Chapter 29, Securities Regulation and Accountant's Legal Responsibility.)

V. Rights of shareholders.

A. Preemptive rights of shareholders.
   1. A preemptive right is the right to purchase a pro rata share of every offering of stock by the corporation in order to preserve each shareholder's proportionate interest in the corporation.
   2. Right may be limited or denied by the articles of incorporation.

B. Shareholders' right to attend meetings and vote.
   1. Shareholders have one vote per share of stock.
   2. Shareholders may usually vote by proxy.
      a. A proxy is a delegation of voting authority, revocable at any time.

     b.   Proxy valid for eleven months unless a shorter period is stated in the proxy.

   3.   Cumulative voting is the right of a shareholder to have as many votes as shares multiplied by the number of directors to be elected; the votes may be cast among candidates in any proportion. Not recognized in all states.

   4.   A voting trust is an irrevocable transfer of stock to a trustee for purpose of voting control.

     a.   Former shareholders are issued certificates of beneficial interest, which are about the same as the beneficial interest in stock ownership except for voting rights.

     b.   Usually the duration of a voting trust is limited by statute to no more than ten years.

     c.   Voting trusts are valid so long as the purpose of the trust is not unlawful.

C.   Shareholders' right to share in dividends.

   1.   Declaration of dividends is solely at the discretion of the board of directors.

   2.   Once validity declared, dividends become a debt of the corporation.

   3.   Distribution can be forced when directors abuse their discretion. For example:

     a.   Diversion of earnings to noncorporate purposes is a good basis for forcing distribution.

     b.   Evidence that surplus is more than adequate is a basis for relief.

     c.   Arbitrary withholding to freeze out shareholders is a basis for relief.

D.   Shareholders' right to information.

   1.   Entitled to financial statements upon written request.

   2.   Right to inspect books may be absolute or for a proper purpose, depending upon local statute. Generally, must have been a shareholder for six months or hold 5 percent of the outstanding shares.

E.   Upon dissolution of the corporation, the claims of creditors are first satisfied and the remaining assets are distributable among its shareholders.

F.   Right to receivership and dissolution where:

   1.   Directors are deadlocked in voting power.

   2.   Acts of directors are illegal, fraudulent, oppressive.

   3.   Corporate assets are being wasted or misapplied.

   4.   Shareholders are deadlocked in voting power.

G.   Right of defrauded subscriber: A subscriber who was

induced by fraud or misrepresentation to subscribe for the stock can cancel the subscription upon discovery.

VI.   Liability of shareholders.

A.   May be personally liable if corporation is used as a device to defraud.
B.   Liable for any unpaid subscription contract.
C.   Liable for any discount where original issue stock sold for less than par.
D.   Liable for illegal dividends or other distributions:
   1.   If corporation is solvent, liable only if illegality is known.
   2.   If corporation is insolvent, liable absolutely.

VII.   Creditors' rights.

A.   Secured creditors can look to their security for payment.
B.   Watered stock: Subsequent creditors can sue the shareholders for the amount of the "water."
C.   Have a receiver appointed if:
   1.   Corporation is unable to pay its debts as they mature, and
   2.   Creditors' claims have been reduced to judgment and returned unsatisfied.
D.   Creditors who also owe unpaid stock subscriptions have no right of setoff.
E.   Creditors have no right to participate in the management of the corporation.
F.   If salary claims of officers and directors are excessive, creditors will be given a priority in bankruptcy proceedings.

Foreign Corporations 28

I. Domestic and foreign corporations.

    A. Domestic corporations are those formed under the law of the state in which they operate.

    B. Foreign corporations are those formed in one state and doing business in another state; they are foreign to the state in which they do business.

    C. Except for acts in interstate commerce, a corporation may not transact business in a state other than the state of its incorporation without the permission and authorization of such state.

    D. The reasoning of the United States Supreme Court in justification for excluding or imposing conditions upon foreign corporations by a state is based upon two theories:

        1. Since the laws of a state have no extraterritorial force in another state, except by comity, a corporation organized in one state does not exist in another unless the latter chooses to recognize it.

        2. Since a corporation is a nonphysical entity, it is not a citizen and therefore not entitled to do business in other states under the "privileges and immunities" clause of the constitution.

    E. Foreign corporation must obtain certificate of authority before it can transact business within the state.

II. Constitutional limitations on the power to exclude or impose conditions.

    A. State regulations of foreign corporations which unduly burden interstate or foreign commerce are unconstitutional under the commerce clause.

    B. As a condition of admission of a foreign corporation, a state may not exact surrender of a privilege guaranteed under the constitution, such as:

        1. Prohibit resort to federal courts.

        2. Deny due process or equal protection of law.

        3. Impair the obligation of contract.

117

C. Retaliatory statutes imposing upon corporations of another state the burdens and restrictions imposed by the latter on foreign corporations doing business in that state have usually been held constitutional.

III. Qualification procedures generally.

A. Must file articles of incorporation with the secretary of state of foreign state.
B. Must name an agent upon whom service of process may be served in the foreign state. In some states this is the secretary of state.
C. A filing and license fee must be paid.
D. Must designate and maintain an office in the foreign state.
E. Must file annual reports with the foreign state.
F. Failure to comply with these requirements justifies the foreign state in denying the corporation the right of access to its courts and enforcing other statutory penalties.

IV. What constitutes doing business within a state?

A. There is a difference between doing business *in* a state and doing business *within* a state.
   1. Doing business in a state involves acts of interstate commerce.
   2. A foreign corporation is doing business within a state when some part of its business, substantial and continuous in character, not merely casual or occasional, is transacted within the state.
B. There is no absolute definition of what constitutes doing business within a state. The courts decide on the facts and circumstances of each case. The following have been held *not* to be doing business within a state:
   1. Mail order: Goods ordered by mail and shipped from without the state.
   2. Salespeople, resident or traveling, who take orders on sample or display, goods being shipped upon order from without the state.
   3. Sale of machinery, plant, or equipment within or without the state, construction or erection of which requires supervision or technical skill in erection; if such skill is not available within the state, the furnishing of such skill is not doing business.
   4. Prosecution, maintenance, and defending lawsuits or other legal proceedings.

5. Collection of debts, accepting evidence of security therefor or compromise and adjustment thereof, including leasing or selling property taken in payment of a debt which did not arise out of a doing business transaction.

6. Appointment of any agent to transact future business or doing acts preliminary to engaging in future business.

7. Doing acts relating solely to management or control of internal corporate affairs.

8. Acquiring or holding stock of a domestic corporation unless such corporation is controlled as an agent.

9. Acceptance of duties as a trustee under a deed of trust, unless for purposes of development or management for profit.

10. Acquire, own, or dispose of real estate for profit, unless the corporation uses, develops, exploits, or manages such property for profit.

C. A series of acts in one state by a foreign corporation, each insufficient by itself to constitute doing business within that state, may constitute doing business within that state when looked at in total.

V. Consequences of not obtaining a certificate of authority when required to do so.

A. May be a misdemeanor punishable by a fine.

B. Denial of the right to continue doing business until compliance.

C. All contracts made within the state are unenforceable by the foreign corporation until there is compliance.

D. In a few states, all contracts made within the state are void and unenforceable by the foreign corporation even after compliance.

VI. Although contracts may be declared unenforceable, as in Part C above, or void, as in Part D above, the contracts are enforceable by the other contracting party regardless of the noncompliance.

29 Securities Regulation And Accountant's Legal Responsibility

I. Objectives of federal securities regulation.

    A. Provide public with accurate, adequate financial and other information upon which to make investment decisions.

    B. Prohibit fraud and manipulation in the sale of securities and for other purposes.

II. Definition of security.

    A. By statute: Any interest or instrument commonly known as a security.

    B. By case law: The subjection of the investor's money to the risk of an enterprise over which he or she exercises no managerial control; the expectation of profit solely from the efforts of others.

III. Public offerings.

    A. Securities Act of 1933, administered by Securities and Exchange Commission since 1934, is applicable federal law.

    B. Registration statement.

        1. Must be filed with SEC by issuer before securities are offered to public.

        2. Content.

            a. Description of registrant's properties and business.

            b. Description of significant provisions of security to be offered and its relationship to registrant's other capital securities.

            c. Information about the management of registrant.

            d. Financial statements certified by independent public accountants.

        3. Statement examined by SEC. If incomplete or inaccurate, registrant informed by letter and required to make amendments (informal letter process).

        4. If deficiencies cannot be corrected by letter process or stem from deliberate attempt to conceal and mislead, SEC holds hearing and may issue stop order.

C. Prospectus.
1. Contains information set forth in registration statement.
2. Must be furnished to prospective investors.
D. Exemptions from registration.
1. Private offerings to a limited number of persons who have access to information and do not propose to re-distribute.
2. Offerings restricted to residents of state where issuing company is organized and doing business.
3. Securities of governmental instrumentalities, charitable institutions, banks, and carriers regulated by ICC.
4. Offerings not in excess of $1,500,000. Notification must be filed with SEC regional office, and offering circular containing certain basic information must be used.
5. Offerings of small business investment companies.
E. Civil liabilities: Persons acquiring security and suffering a loss because of false statements or improper omissions in registration statement may sue for losses sustained. Persons liable:
1. Signers of registration statement.
2. Directors and partners of issuer.
3. Persons named in registration statement with consent as about to become directors or partners.
4. Accountants, engineers, appraisers, and underwriters.
F. Defenses.
1. Due diligence defense: No person, other than issuer, is liable in regard to any part of registration statement:
a. Purporting to be made on the authority of an expert (other than the person), if the person had no reasonable ground to believe and did not believe, at the time registration statement became effective, that statements therein were untrue or that there was an omission to state a material fact required to be stated therein or necessary to make the statements therein not misleading.
b. Not purporting to be made on the authority of an expert, if the person had, after reasonable investigation, reasonable ground to believe, and did believe, that statements therein were true and that there was no omission of a material fact required to be stated therein or necessary to make statements therein not misleading.
2. Causation defense: Cause of damages of person

acquiring security are other than false statements or omissions in registration statement.

IV. Public trading.

    A. Securities Exchange Act of 1934 is applicable federal law. Extended disclosure requirements to securities listed on national stock exchanges. Amendment of 1964 made requirements applicable to over-the-counter market.

    B. Registration application.

        1. Must be filed with exchange and SEC as a condition of listing and registration for public trading.

            a. National securities markets.

            b. Over-the-counter markets, if assets exceed $1 million and shareholders number 500 or more.

        2. Nature and content prescribed (like public offering statement); certified financial statements must be included.

    C. Reports.

        1. Annual reports; Form 10–K; certified financial statements.

        2. Quarterly reports; Form 10–Q, unaudited.

        3. Form 8–K, filed whenever certain significant events occur.

V. Proxy and tender offer solicitations.

    A. Proxy: Delegation of right to vote.

        1. Instructed proxy: Stockholder specifies how proxy is to to vote.

        2. May be for election of directors or other action.

        3. Disclosure must be made of all material facts, including names and interests of participants in proxy contest.

        4. Proxy material must be filed with SEC in advance.

        5. Stockholders must be able to vote yes or no.

    B. Tender offer: Proposed acquisition of a company's equity securities for purpose of gaining control; take-over bid.

        1. Williams Act, 1968 amendment to Securities Exchange Act: Reporting and disclosure requirements extended to planned acquisitions in excess of 10 percent.

        2. Amendment of 1970 reduced amount to 5 percent.

        3. Applies to tender offers and direct purchases and to persons soliciting acceptance or rejection.

VI.   Insider trading.

    A. Regulations apply to officers, directors, and beneficial owners of 10 percent of registered equity securities of registered companies.

    B. Initial report showing holdings of equity securities must be filed.

    C. Periodic reports must be filed for any month holdings change.

    D. Company can recover gains made from purchases and sales within six-month period. Stockholders may sue on behalf of company.

    E. May not make short sales.

VII. Fraudulent interstate transactions. In interstate commerce, unlawful in the offer or sale of securities to:

    A. Employ device, scheme, or artifice to defraud.

    B. Obtain money or property by untrue statements or omissions causing offeree or buyer to be misled.

    C. Engage in practice which operates as fraud or deceit upon purchaser.

    D. Circulate a communication about a security for a consideration without revealing such consideration and the amount thereof.

VIII. Public accountant–client relationship.

    A. Public accountant as an independent contractor.

        1. Contracts to render an agreed performance for the employer.

        2. Does not act on the employer's behalf.

        3. Has no authority to deal with third persons or to affect the employer's contractual relations with third persons.

        4. Manner of performance is not subject to any right of control by the employer.

        5. Relationship between public accountant and client is of a personal character and, therefore, accountant cannot delegate duties to another accountant without consent of the client.

    B. Cannot give legal advice or answer legal questions completely unrelated to the work of auditing books and preparing tax returns.

    C. Must communicate to the client the information obtained

in an audit or other work that is a full, fair, and complete disclosure consistent with responsibility to the client.

1. Any misrepresentation is negligence, and accountant is liable to client for damage proximately caused by negligence.

2. What constitutes a fair disclosure will be determined by a lay person's standard established by the jury.

D. Absent an agreement to the contrary, the working papers belong to the accountant, not to the client.

1. This is confidential information and cannot be transferred or disclosed to another without the client's consent. This rule also applies to other confidential communications with client.

2. In majority of states and in federal courts, working papers and other confidential communications are not privileged communications; therefore, they are subject to legal process and must be produced or disclosed in proper court proceedings.

IX. Public accountant's common law liability to third persons.

A. Contractual liability.

1. General rule: Only persons who are in privity of contract with the accountant can recover for breach of the accountant's duty of performance of the contract. This includes ordinary negligence of the accountant.

2. Principal exception: Third party beneficiary of the contract. If third party was intended beneficiary of the contract and accountant had knowledge of this, then third party has standing to sue for losses caused by accountant's negligence.

B. Tort liability (fraud).

1. Third person may recover from accountant if accountant is guilty of actual or constructive fraud.

   a. Actual fraud is a misstatement of a material fact with intent to mislead.

   b. Constructive fraud is a misstatement of a material fact without actual intent, but with reckless disregard for the truth.

      (1) Gross negligence is constructive fraud.

      (2) Gross negligence is an extreme departure from the ordinary standard of care.

   c. Proof required.

      (1) Knowledge of falsity or gross negligence.

      (2) Reasonable reliance on falsity by injured party.

      (3) Damages proximately caused by falsity.

X. Public accountant's liability under the Securities Act and the Securities Exchange Act.

A. The Securities Act eliminates privity defense against a third party investor.

1. If the financial statement in the registration statement contains a material false statement or misleading omission due to accountant's lack of due diligence (ordinary negligence), then accountant is liable to all purchasers of the securities.

2. Purchaser. Plaintiff need prove only two facts:

a. That he or she purchased the security.

b. That the certified financial statement contained a false statement or omission of a material fact.

3. Shifts burden of proof to accountant.

a. Must prove he or she did not act negligently or fraudulently.

b. Standard of care is that required of a prudent person in the management of his or her own property.

4. Accountant's duty of care extends beyond the date of the financial statement up to the date when the registration statement becomes effective.

5. Plaintiff must institute action within one year after discovery of the untrue statement or omission, but in no event more than three years after the sale.

B. Under the Securities Exchange Act, accountant may be liable to any person who bought or sold securities at a price which was affected by reliance on a false or misleading financial statement certified by the accountant and filed with the SEC.

1. Burden is on accountant to prove that he or she acted in good faith and had no knowledge that the financial statement was false or misleading.

2. Plaintiff must institute action within one year after discovery of the false or misleading statement, but in no event more than three years after the sale.

XI. Public accountant's criminal liability.

A. The Securities Act of 1933 and the Securities Exchange Act of 1934.

1. Provide for criminal penalties for a willful violation of the acts.

2. A fine of not more than $10,000 or imprisonment for not more than five years or both may be imposed.

B. The Internal Revenue Code as well as other federal and state statutes also provide for criminal penalties for willfully making or certifying false reports.

PART SEVEN
Personal Property
and Bailments

Personal Property 30

I. Concepts of property.

   A. Intangible concept in its technical legal sense signifies rights, privileges, and powers in relation to tangible and intangible things as distinguished from things themselves.
   B. Popular meaning of the term refers to the things themselves which may be the subject of ownership.
      1. It designates the subject matter to which the rights, privileges and powers themselves attach.
      2. It includes both tangibles and intangibles.

II. Personal property as distinguished from real property.

   A. Conveyance.
      1. Real property must be conveyed by formal instrument.
      2. Personal property may be transferred by delivery or a simple informal writing.
   B. Under Statute of Frauds, enforceability of the contracts relating to two types of property differ.
   C. Usually only real property is subject to right of dower and curtesy.
   D. Judgments are liens only on real estate.
   E. The two types are subject to different tax laws.

III. Property classified.

   A. Every type of property not real is personal.
      1. Real property is land or anything permanently attached to land.
      2. When term real property designates ownership in land it is limited to estates of freehold.
         a. An estate of inheritance.
         b. An estate for life.
   B. Personal property.
      1. Chattels real: An estate in real property at will, from year to year or for a term of years, is personal property.

127

2. Chattels personal corporeal: Interests in things move-able.
   a. Growing trees when subject to an ownership distinct from the soil.
   b. Growing crops, the annual produce of labor and cultivation of the earth.
3. Chattels personal incorporeal: Interests in intangible property (choses in action), such as, contract rights, claims arising out of torts, promissory notes, corporate stock and patents.

IV. Fixtures are personalty converted into realty.

A. Tests to determine conversion of personalty to realty.
   1. Intention test.
      a. The law presumes a tenant's annexations are made to be detached if no injury results.
      b. The law presumes an owner's annexations have been made for greater enjoyment of the realty.
      c. The law presumes a mortgagor's annexations are made to enhance the value of the property.
   2. Mode of annexation: It must not merely be essential to the use of the structure but must be attached or mechanically fitted to constitute a part of the structure itself.
   3. Mode of adaptation: The relationship of the object to the purpose of the structure.
B. Trade fixtures: Fixtures added to the leasehold by a tenant used in the tenant's trade or business.
   1. Presumption is that the tenant intends to remove them at end of lease.
   2. Generally can be removed unless removal will cause serious injury to leasehold.
   3. Must be removed before expiration of lease.

V. Severance.

A. Part of the realty may be converted into personalty when there is an intention to do so. However, mere detachment without intention does not convert realty into personalty.
B. Crops.
   1. As between grantor and grantee, growing crops are regarded as realty unless reserved as personalty in the deed.
   2. Crops planted by owner are often considered realty, while those planted by tenant are personalty as to the land owner, but realty as to all others.

VI. Ways of acquiring title.
- A. Title in things not owned.
  1. Occupation of land.
  2. Reducing wild animals to possession or control.
  3. Taking abandoned property.
  4. Copyrights and patents.
     - a. Copyright good for a lifetime plus fifty years.
     - b. Patent good for seventeen years.
  5. Ideas. Nonpermissive use compensable if:
     - a. Idea is novel,
     - b. Reduced to concrete form, and
     - c. Disclosed with indication that compensation is expected.
- B. Title by transfer.
  1. Judgment:
     - a. *In rem*: Judgment against the thing. Result of foreclosure, probate and similar actions.
     - b. *In personam*: Judgment against a person. May be satisfied out of person's property.
  2. Sale and gift.
     - a. Deeds and bill of sale.
     - b. Gifts *inter vivos*: Gifts between living persons.
        - (1) Intent to divest oneself absolutely.
        - (2) Must be actual or constructive delivery.
        - (3) Must be accepted.
     - c. Gift *causa mortis*: Made in contemplation of death, a conditional gift absolute in form with delivery, actual or constructive, to donee. Gift defeated if:
        - (1) Contemplated danger of death passes.
        - (2) Death results from a cause other than that which is contemplated (intervening cause).
        - (3) Donor revokes it before death.
        - (4) Donee dies before donor.
  3. By will, law of descent, or succession.
- C. Title by accession.
  1. Loss of identity test.
     - a. Repair labor lost in object repaired.
     - b. Materials furnished absorb labor.
     - c. Ownership passes to innocent taker if identity lost, but not to willful taker unless increase in value is extraordinary. Original owner has right to value of property at time of taking.
  2. Relative value test: Party who contributes greater value has title.

3. Principal and accessory test: Party who owns principal chattel has title.
4. Improvement by thief.
   a. Chattel in its improved state belongs to owner of original chattel.
   b. Owner of original may retake chattel in improved state from innocent purchaser from thief.
5. Improvement by an innocent purchaser from a thief.
   a. If the improvement is substantial, the innocent purchaser acquires a right to the goods subject to a duty to compensate the true owner for the original value.

D. Title by finding.
   1. Lost property.
      a. Owner has unknowingly parted with possession through carelessness.
      b. Finder may retain it as gratuitous bailee for true owner.
      c. Exceptions: Occupier of premises has superior right to possession over a trespasser and over the finder of goods embedded in the ground.
   2. Mislaid property.
      a. Owner has knowingly laid property in a place with the intention of picking it up or retaking possession of it at a later time but has forgotten where it is.
      b. Occupier of premises where it is found has right to hold it as a gratuitous bailee for the true owner.
      c. Exception: Finder of treasure trove, i.e., bullion or coin found in the ground, has a claim superior to that of the owner of the land.

E. Confusion of goods: Intermixture of fungible goods of different owners.
   1. Innocent confusion: Each owner acquires a proportionate undivided interest in the entire mass. Losses spread among all owners proportionately.
   2. Wrongful confusion: Wrongdoer loses his or her interest in mass until he or she can prove interest and absorbs all losses.

Bailments 31

I. Definition: A transfer of possession of personal property from one person, called the bailor, to another, called the bailee, upon a contract, expressed or implied, to be held by the latter according to the purpose of the transfer and returned or delivered over after the purpose is accomplished.

II. Characteristics.

A. Physical transfer of possession into the control of bailee. Note: It is the lack of this characteristic that prevents cars parked in a parking lot without the keys being left with the attendant from becoming bailments. However, exercise of other physical controls may be a factor.

B. An intention on the part of the bailee to receive the personal property as the subject matter of bailment. Note: It is the lack of this characteristic that prevents clothing hung on cloak racks and items in pockets of "checked" clothing (things within things) from becoming bailments.

C. Retention of title by the bailor.

D. Return of the property to the bailor or delivery over of the property to a third person, as the bailor directs. The nature of the transaction continues to be a bailment even if the form of the property is changed, so long as the identical items are returned or delivered over, that is to say, so long as the identity of the items may be traced through the transaction.

III. Types of bailments and degrees of care required.

A. Bailment for sole benefit of bailor: Slight care.

B. Mutual benefit bailment: Ordinary care.

C. Bailment for sole benefit of bailee: Extraordinary care.

D. The above standards of care will vary according to the value and character of the property involved.

IV. Liability of bailee.

    A. If property is returned to bailor in damaged condition or if bailee is unable to return property as required by contract, bailee has burden of showing he or she used degree of care required under type of bailment involved.

    B. Bailee is liable for loss sustained by bailor if he or she:

       1. Failed to exercise the degree of care required or

       2. Exceeded the terms of the bailment (in which case bailee becomes an insurer of the bailed property) or

       3. Agrees to insure the goods against certain risks but fails to do so (absolute liability for any loss from the contemplated risks) or

       4. Returns the property to the wrong person.

    C. Bailment contracts against required care.

       1. Provisions limiting liability disfavored by the law. Must be absolutely clear and communicated before contract entered into.

       2. Illegal in many states as against public policy in case of professional bailees, i.e., firms in which bailment is an incident of their business.

V. Liability of the bailor.

    A. Mutual benefit bailments: Must use reasonable care to determine that property is reasonably fit for purpose intended.

    B. Bailments for sole benefit of bailee: Must advise bailee of known defects.

VI. Bailee's rights.

    A. A bailee who agrees to perform work upon or render services in connection with the bailed goods is entitled to reasonable compensation, including reimbursement for expenses which are incident to his or her performance.

       1. The bailee has a lien upon the goods for the services or materials as long as the goods remain in his or her possession.

    B. Unless otherwise agreed, a bailee who is using the bailed goods for personal benefit bears all the ordinary expenses of maintenance incident to the normal use. The bailor, however, bears the cost of all extraordinary repairs and replacements that are not normally incident to the use.

VII. Common carriers of goods.

    A. Strict liability: A common carrier is treated as an insurer of

the safety of the goods, subject to the following exceptions:
1. Acts of God.
2. Acts of public enemy.
3. Acts or negligence of the shipper.
4. Inherent nature of the goods.
5. Act of public authority.

(This strict liability applies only during actual carriage of the goods).

B. Limitation of liability.
1. Common carrier can limit its liability by contract with the shipper by offering the shipper a choice between limited and unlimited liability at different shipping rates.
2. Shipper must assent to limitation.

VIII. Common carriers of passengers.

A. Common carrier does not have strict liability as in the case of goods, but is held to a very high degree of care.
B. Baggage not retained by the passenger is treated the same as goods above. Strict liability.

32 Documents of Title

I. Definitions.

    A. Document of title: Includes bill of lading, dock warrant, dock receipt, warehouse receipt or order for the delivery of goods, and also any other document which in the regular course of business or financing is treated as adequately evidencing that the person in possession of it is entitled to receive, hold, and dispose of the document and the goods it covers.

    B. Warehouse receipt: A receipt issued by a person engaged in the business of storing goods for hire.

    C. Bill of lading: A document evidencing the receipt of goods for shipment issued by a person engaged in the business of transporting or forwarding goods.

II. Warehouse receipts.

    A. Must contain the location, date, number, person to receive the goods, rates, description of goods, signature of warehouseman, whether or not warehouseman is owner, and a statement of advances made or liabilities incurred for which the warehouseman claims a lien or security interest.

    B. The warehouseman is liable to a bona fide purchaser for value of the document for damages caused by nonreceipt or misdescription of the goods, unless the document conspicuously indicates that the issuer does not know whether the goods or any part of them were in fact received or whether they conform to the description in kind, quantity, or condition.

    C. Unless the warehouse receipt otherwise provides, a warehouseman must keep separate the goods covered by each receipt so as to permit at all times identification and delivery of those goods, except that different lots of fungible goods may be commingled where authorized by agreement or custom.

    D. A buyer in the ordinary course of business of fungible goods sold and delivered by a warehouseman who is also in the business of buying and selling such goods takes them free of any claim under a warehouse receipt even though it has been duly negotiated.

E. Where a blank in a negotiable warehouse receipt has been filled in without authority, a purchaser for value and without notice of the want of authority may treat the insertion as authorized. Any other unauthorized alteration leaves any receipt enforceable against the issuer according to its original tenor (wording before alteration).

F. The warehouseman has a lien on the goods for the payment of his charges and necessary expenses in connection with keeping and handling the goods.

III. Bills of lading.

A. Carrier is liable to the consignee for nonreceipt or misdescription the same as the warehouseman in Part B of II above.

B. An unauthorized alteration or filling in of a blank in a bill of lading leaves the bill enforceable according to its original tenor.

C. The issuer of a through bill of lading is liable to the holder of the document for loss or damage to the goods caused by any connecting or delivering carrier. The liability of the connecting carrier is limited to the period while the goods are in its possession.

D. Instead of issuing a bill of lading to the consignor at the place of shipment, a carrier may at the request of the consignor procure the bill to be issued at destination or at any other place designated in the request.

E. The carrier has a lien on the goods for the payment of charges and necessary expenses in connection with carrying and preserving the goods.

IV. Negotiation and transfer.

A. A document of title is negotiable if by its terms the goods are to be delivered to bearer or to the order of a named person. Any other document is nonnegotiable.

B. A negotiable document of title is "duly negotiated" when it is negotiated to a holder who purchases it in good faith, without notice of any defense against or claim to it on the part of any person, and for value, unless it is established that the negotiation is not in the regular course of business or financing or involves receiving the document in settlement or payment of a money obligation.

    C. Rights acquired by due negotiation.
1. Title to the document and the goods, if transferor had title.
2. Right to goods delivered to the bailee after the issuance of the document.
3. The direct obligation of the issuer to hold or deliver the goods according to the terms of the document.
4. Take title and rights free of most defenses, similar to a holder in due course of negotiable instruments.

V. Rights acquired in the absence of due negotiation.

    A. Transferee acquires the title and rights which the transferor had or had actual authority to convey.

    B. If the document is nonnegotiable, the transferee acquires the direct obligation of the bailee to hold possession of the goods for him or her according to the terms of the document, upon giving notice to the bailee of the transfer. Prior to such notification, the title of the transferee to the goods may be defeated by:
1. A levy upon or an attachment of the goods by a creditor of the transferor of the document or
2. Notice to the bailee of a subsequent sale of the goods by the transferor.

VI. Liability of carrier or warehouseman.

    A. A bailee who in good faith including observance of reasonable commercial standards has received goods and delivered or otherwise disposed of them according to the terms of the document of title is not liable therefor.

    B. This rule applies even though the person to whom bailee delivered the goods had no authority to receive them.

VII. Warranties.

    A. A person who negotiates or transfers a document of title for value warrants to the immediate purchaser only:
1. That the document is genuine.
2. That he or she has no knowledge of any fact which would impair its validity or worth.
3. That the negotiation or transfer is rightful and fully effective with respect to the title to the document and the goods it represents.

    B. The indorsement of a document of title issued by a bailee does not make the indorser liable for any default by the bailee or by previous indorsers.

PART EIGHT
Sales and
Products Liability

The Sales Contract 33

I. Uniform Commercial Code, Article 2, Sales, as modified and adopted by state legislatures and interpreted by state courts, is applicable law.

A. Common law of contracts applies in absence of appropriate UCC provisions.
B. Special UCC provisions for merchant sellers and buyers.
  1. Purpose: Facilitate commercial transactions and hold merchants to higher standard of dealings.
  2. Merchants defined as dealers in the goods or those who hold themselves or their agents out as having knowledge or skill peculiar to the goods or practices involved.

II. The nature of a sale.

A. Definition: A sale is the transfer of title (ownership) of goods (personal property) from a seller to a buyer for a consideration, known as the price.
B. Title.
  1. Right to goods superior to all others.
    a. Right may be enforced by replevin action, and/or damages may be had in tort for another's wrongful nonpermissive use of titleholder's property by action for conversion.
    b. If debtor's title can be established, judgment creditors can levy upon or attach goods of their judgment debtors.
  2. Absolute title: One interest only.
    a. Individual: Interest in one person only.
    b. Joint: Joint tenancy or tenancy in common.
  3. Divided title: Legal title in one or more persons, equitable title or security interest in another or others.
C. Goods.
  1. Goods are defined as all things (including specially manufactured goods) which are movable at the time of identification to the contract for sale.

139

    2.   Includes unborn young of animals; growing crops and timber; minerals and structures to be removed from realty by the seller; and undivided shares in identified bulks of fungible goods.

    3.   Excludes money (as currency), investment securities, things in action, and bulk sales (not in the ordinary course of business).

D. Price.

    1.   While usually payable in money, price may be payable in goods or any other thing of value.

    2.   If payable in goods, buyer is treated as a seller of the goods used in payment, and his or her rights and duties are governed by UCC, Article 2, Sales.

E. Sales distinguished from:

    1.   Gifts: Transfer of title without consideration.

    2.   Bailments: Transfer of possession only.

    3.   Consignments: Transfer of possession with power in transferee to give good title to third person.

    4.   Security interests.

        a.   Conditional sale: Seller retains legal title as security interest; buyer has equitable title.

        b.   Chattel mortgage: Buyer or borrower grants security interest to seller or lender.

        c.   Pledge: Transfer of possession and security interest.

III. Sales contract.

A. Present sales.

    1.   Goods must be both existing and identified.

    2.   When title passes depends upon agreement of the parties with respect to physical delivery of the goods and delivery of documents to title, if any.

B. Sales of part interests.

    1.   There may be a sale of a part interest in existing identified goods.

    2.   A share in identified bulk of fungible goods (like grade and quality) may be sold though the total quantity of bulk is undetermined.

    3.   Buyer becomes tenant in common.

C. Contracts to sell goods at a future time.

    1.   Involve goods which are not both existing and identified.

    2.   Buyer obtains a special property and an insurable interest when the goods are shipped, marked, or otherwise identified to the contract (see Chapter 34).

D. Offer and acceptance.
  1. Offer need not include all terms to result in contract if parties so intended. Agreement does not fail for indefiniteness if court can determine appropriate remedy.
  2. Signed, written offers by merchant buyers and sellers providing definite duration (firm offer) may not be revoked before time stated, not to exceed three months.
  3. Offers may be accepted in any manner and by any medium reasonable in the circumstances.
  4. Offers to buy goods may be accepted by promises to ship or by shipment of conforming or nonconforming goods. If nonconforming, not treated as acceptance if seller notified buyer shipment is offered as accommodation.
  5. Acceptance is effective even though additional terms are stated.
     a. Additional terms treated as proposals.
     b. Between merchants, additional terms become part of contract unless they:
        (1) Materially alter offer,
        (2) Are objected to by offeror, or
        (3) Were prohibited by terms of offer.
  6. Conduct on the part of both parties recognizing the existence of a contract is sufficient to show agreement between them.
E. Open price term. Price is the reasonable price if:
  1. Nothing is said as to price,
  2. The price is left to be agreed upon but the parties fail to agree, or
  3. A market or other standard was to be used but failed to become available.
F. Statute of Frauds.
  1. Applies to contracts for the sale of goods for a price of $500 or more.
  2. Statute may be satisfied by:
     a. Delivery and acceptance of all or part of the goods to the extent of the amount delivered and accepted.
     b. Payment of all or part of the price to the extent of the payment made.
     c. Note or memorandum signed by party to be charged or party's agent. Writing must:
        (1) Evidence contract for sale of goods,
        (2) Be signed—any symbol intended to authenticate, and
        (3) Specify quantity.

        d. Between merchants, confirmatory memo satisfies Statute of Frauds unless objected to in ten days.

    3. Contracts for specially manufactured goods are enforceable without compliance if seller has commenced manufacture or made commitments to procure goods.

G. Unconscionable contracts or clauses.

    1. Enforcement would result in oppression or unfair surprise; offends conscience of the court.

    2. Court may, as matter of law, find contract or any clause unconscionable at time it was made.

    3. Court may:

        a. Refuse to enforce contract.

        b. Enforce remainder of contract without the unconscionable clause.

        c. Limit application of clause to avoid unconscionable result.

    4. Parties may give evidence of commercial setting, purpose, and effect to aid court's determination.

IV.   Bulk transfers.

A. Law applies to transfers of a major part of inventory not in the ordinary course of business. Does not apply to equipment transfers unless in connection with inventory transfer.

B. Businesses affected are those whose principal business is selling merchandise from stock. Includes those who manufacture own stock.

C. Purpose.

    1. To protect creditors of the seller: Bulk transfer is ineffective against creditors of seller unless law is complied with.

    2. Buyer, as well as purchasers from buyer who do not pay value or know of noncompliance, take property subject to defect in title.

    3. Purchasers from buyer who acquire goods for value, in good faith, and without notice of noncompliance get good title.

D. Statutory requirements.

    1. Transferee must require transferor to furnish list of transferor's creditors. List must:

        a. Contain names and addresses of all creditors and amounts owed, including disputed claims.

        b. Be signed and sworn to.

    2. Parties must prepare a schedule of property to be transferred.

3. List and schedule must be preserved for six months following transfer and be available for inspection or must be filed in a public office as designated by state statute.
4. Notice to creditors.
   a. Must be given at least ten days prior to taking possession of the goods or payment of the price, whichever happens first.
   b. Must state that transfer is to occur, names and addresses of transferor and transferee, and whether debts are to be paid when due. If debts are not to be so paid, notice must also state details of transaction, including time and place of payment of consideration for bulk transfer.
   c. Must be delivered personally or by registered or certified mail.
E. Penal provision: Seller making a false or incomplete answer to inquiries of purchaser is guilty of misdemeanor.
F. Benefits derived by creditors.
   1. If statute complied with, creditors can garnish sum due seller from purchaser.
   2. If statute not complied with, defense of lack of privity overcome by creditors of seller in action against purchaser, since law provides that purchaser who fails to conform with statutory requirements is accountable to creditors of seller for goods coming into his or her possession by virtue of sale or assignment.
G. Special provisions for auction sales make auctioneer liable for compliance with the bulk transfer law.

34 Title and Property Rights in Goods

I. Title.

    A. Refers to ownership.

    B. Location of title is significant with respect to:
        1. Rights of action for replevin and conversion.
        2. Statutory and common law ownership liabilities.
        3. Rights of judgment creditors of seller and buyer.

    C. Other rights which are, or may be, independent of title:
        1. Special property.
        2. Insurable interest.
        3. Right to the goods.
        4. Security interest.

II. Passage of title.

    A. Where the parties have expressly agreed when title shall pass, it passes in accordance with their agreement.

    B. Where the parties have not expressly agreed when title shall pass, it passes as follows for present sales (existing and identified goods), as follows:
        1. If delivery is to be made without moving the goods and no documents are to be delivered, it passes at the time of contracting.
        2. If delivery is to be made without moving the goods and the seller is to deliver a document of title, title passes at the time when and the place where seller delivers such documents.
        3. If the seller is obligated to send the goods but not deliver them, title passes at the time and place of shipment, i.e., when goods are placed in hands of carrier.
        4. If the seller is obligated to deliver the goods, title passes at time of tender at the destination.
        Note: Where goods are to be sent or delivered, title passes as above stated even though a security interest has been reserved and/or a document of title is to be delivered at a definite time and place.

III. Revesting title in seller.

    A. By rejection or refusal of the buyer to receive or retain the goods, justified or unjustified.

    B. By revocation of acceptance of nonconforming goods if buyer accepted the goods:

        1. Reasonably assuming nonconformity would be cured and it was not reasonably cured or

        2. Without discovery of nonconformity due to:

            a. Difficulty of discovery before acceptance or

            b. Seller's assurances.

        3. Seller must be notified:

            a. Within reasonable time after discovery of nonconformity and

            b. Before substantial change in condition of goods not due to their own defects.

        4. Title revests after notice to seller.

IV. Voidable title and good faith purchasers.

    A. Voidable title is one acquired under circumstances which permit the former owner to rescind the transfer and re-acquire title.

    B. Holder of voidable title can pass good title to a good faith (innocent) purchaser for value and thereby cut off all rights of the former owner in the goods.

    C. The following create a voidable title:

        1. Where the original owner (seller) was deceived as to the identity of the buyer.

        2. Where the seller delivered the goods to the buyer in exchange for a check which was subsequently dishonored.

        3. Where the transaction was a cash sale and the seller delivered the goods to the buyer upon a promise to pay cash immediately, which he or she failed to do.

        4. Where the goods were obtained by fraud, punishable as criminal larceny.

        5. Minor's contracts.

        6. Where the goods were obtained by mistake, duress or undue influence.

V. Estoppel of owner's assertion of title.

    A. Owner who gives possession and indicia of ownership to another is estopped from asserting title against an innocent purchaser for value from the latter.

    B. Where buyer, to whom title has passed, leaves goods in possession of seller and the latter resells and delivers the

goods to an innocent purchaser for value, the second
buyer acquires good title to the goods.

1. Rule applies even where goods were sold to second
buyer under nonnegotiable bill of lading.
2. Rule does not apply where second buyer learns of first
buyer's rights before taking physical possession of
goods. Fact that he or she paid purchase price is immaterial.
3. When seller keeps possession of the goods, the sale is
void as to seller's creditors, except for retention of possession in good faith and in the current course of trade
by a merchant-seller for a reasonable time after a
sale.

C. Possession alone is sufficient to create estoppel where
owner gives possession of goods to a merchant who deals
in goods of that kind.

1. Referred to as *entrusting*.
2. Purchaser from merchant gets good title even if merchant's acquisition or disposition of goods was larce-
nous.

VI. Identification of goods to the contract.

A. Title cannot pass prior to identification of goods to the
contract.
B. Present sales: Identification is made at time contract is
entered into.
C. Contracts to sell goods at a future time: Identification
takes place:

1. Generally, when goods are shipped, marked, or otherwise designated.
2. When animals are conceived, in the case of contracts
to sell unborn animals.
3. When crops are planted, in the case of contracts to sell
future crops.

D. By identification, buyer acquires a special property and
insurable interest in the goods, even though nonconforming, and has option to return and reject.
E. Seller retains an insurable interest in goods as long as he or
she has title or any security interest. Until default, insolvency, or notification to buyer that identification is final,
seller may substitute other goods where identification was
by seller alone.

VII. Nature of buyer's special property.

A. Special property: An interest in goods, distinguished from title, which the buyer has as a result of their identification to the contract.

    B.   The specific rights encompassed by the term *Special property* are:

        1.   Right to goods where seller becomes insolvent within ten days after receipt of the first installment of their price. Where buyer made identification, this right accrues only if goods conform. Tender of unpaid balance required.

        2.   Right to inspect at any reasonable place and time.

        3.   Right to replevin if unable to effect "cover."

        4.   Right to sue third parties for injury, destruction, or conversion of the goods.

        5.   Insurable interest.

VIII.   Insurable interest.

    A.   Before identification, seller alone has title and insurable interest.

    B.   After identification and before title passes, both seller and buyer have insurable interest. Buyer's interest exists even though goods are nonconforming.

    C.   After title passes, buyer only has insurable interest unless seller has security interest.

    D.   Insurable interest carries with it right to proceed against third persons for injury or conversion of goods.

IX.   Security interest.

    A.   An interest in personal property designed to assure payment or performance by buyer.

    B.   Security interest in seller.

        1.   Conditional sales contract: Security interest consists of reservation of title by seller until final installment payment.

        2.   Negotiable bill of lading to seller's order: Carrier is responsible for delivery of goods only as seller directs by virtue of endorsement.

        3.   Nonnegotiable bill of lading naming seller as consignee.

    C.   Security interest in buyer: Buyer who rejects goods or revokes acceptance by reason of nonconformity has possessory lien for payments made or expenses incurred.

35 Risk of Loss

I. Introduction.

   A. Risk of loss deals with the question of who, as between seller and buyer, bears the loss arising from damage, destruction, or disappearance of the goods without fault of either party between the time the contract for sale is entered into and the time title and possession pass to the buyer.

   B. In the absence of proper insurance coverage where the risk is on the seller at the time of the loss, he or she will suffer the loss of the value of the goods; where it is on the buyer, he or she may be required to pay for goods never received.

II. Casualty to goods identified at time of contracting, but before risk of loss passes. Buyer may:

   A. Treat the contract as avoided or

   B. Accept the goods with due allowance from the contract price for deterioration or deficiency in quantity,

   C. But cannot sue the seller for damages for breach of contract.

III. The sales contract may specify who shall bear the risk of loss or it may divide the risk, as the parties see fit.

IV. Risk bearing in absence of agreement, in general.

   A. Where goods are in possession of bailee to be delivered without being moved, risk of loss passes to buyer either on receipt of negotiable document of title or on acknowledgement by bailee of buyer's right to possession or on receipt of nonnegotiable document of title, unless bailee refuses to honor instrument.

   B. Where seller is required to ship by carrier but not required to deliver at a particular destination, risk passes when goods are duly delivered to carrier.

   C. Where seller is required to ship by carrier to a particular

destination, risk passes when goods are tendered as to enable buyer to take delivery from the carrier.
D. If none of above apply to transaction, risk passes on receipt of goods by buyer, if seller is merchant.
E. If none of above apply to transaction, risk passes on tender to buyer if seller is nonmerchant.

V. Risk bearing in event of breach.

A. Breach by seller.
   1. Where goods do not conform so as to give right of rejection to buyer, risk of loss remains on seller until cure or acceptance.
   2. Where buyer rightfully revokes acceptance, he or she may to the extent of deficient insurance coverage treat the risk of loss as having rested on the seller from the beginning.
B. Breach by buyer. Where buyer of conforming goods identified to the contract repudiates or otherwise breaches before risk of loss has passed to him or her, seller may to the extent of any insurance deficiency treat the risk of loss as resting on the buyer for a commercially reasonable time.

VI. Sale on approval and sale or return.

A. Terms apply to sales in which buyer may return goods even though they conform to the contract. Nature of agreement determines when title is transferred and when risk of loss passes.
B. Sale on approval.
   1. Goods delivered primarily for use.
   2. Special incidents.
      a. Not subject to claims of buyer's creditors until acceptance (approval of sale).
      b. Risk of loss and title do not pass to buyer until acceptance.
      c. Failure to notify seller timely of election to return goods is acceptance.
      d. Acceptance of any part is acceptance of the whole.
      e. Return is at seller's risk and expense, after due notice of election to return, but a merchant buyer must follow any reasonable instructions.
C. Sale or return.
   1. Goods are delivered primarily for resale.

      2. Special incidents.
        a. Subject to claims of buyer's creditors while in buyer's possession.
        b. Option to return continues while goods are in substantially original condition; must be seasonably exercised.
        c. Return is at buyer's risk and expense.
      3. Shipments on consignment or on memorandum.
        a. Applies to goods delivered for sale to a person who maintains a place of business where the person deals in goods of the kind involved, under a name other than the name of the person making delivery.
        b. The goods are deemed to be on sale or return with respect to claims of creditors of the person conducting the business unless:
          (1) Consignor's interest is evidenced by a sign or
          (2) Consignee's creditors know consignee is engaged in selling goods of others or
          (3) Appropriate filings are made (see Chapter 44, Secured Transactions).

  VII. Shipping terms.

    A. FOB and FAS shipments.
      1. FOB: Free on board; FAS: Free alongside.
      2. FOB, place of shipment: Seller must bear expense and risk of putting goods into possession of the carrier.
      3. FOB, place of destination: Seller must bear expense and risk of transporting the goods to that place and there tender delivery of them.
      4. FOB, vessel, car, or other vehicle: Seller must bear expense and risk of loading the goods on board.
      5. FAS, vessel in a named port: Seller must bear expense and risk of delivering goods alongside the vessel in that port.
    B. CIF and C&F shipments.
      1. CIF: Price includes cost, insurance, and freight; C&F: Price includes cost and freight only.
      2. CIF: Seller must at his own expense and risk:
        a. Put goods in possession of carrier at port for shipment and obtain negotiable bill of lading.
        b. Load goods and obtain receipt showing prepayment of freight.
        c. Obtain policy of insurance providing for payment of loss to order of buyer.

      d.   Prepare invoice and procure document to effect shipment.

      e.   Forward all documents to buyer.

   3.   C&F: Same as CIF except for obligation as to insurance.

   4.   Both considered shipment, not destination, contracts.

C. Delivery ex-ship. Seller must:

   1.   Discharge all liens arising out of the carriage.

   2.   Furnish buyer with a direction which puts carrier under a duty to deliver goods.

   3.   Neither title nor risk of loss passes until goods leave ship's tackle.

D. No arrival, no sale.

   1.   Seller must ship and tender conforming goods.

   2.   Seller assumes no obligation that goods will arrive unless he or she has caused nonarrival.

   3.   If goods, in part, are lost or deteriorated without seller's fault, buyer may proceed as if there had been casualty to identified goods.

E. COD: Collect on delivery.

   1.   Where buyer agrees to pay freight, title and risk of loss pass upon delivery to carrier.

   2.   COD shipment deprives buyer of right of inspection.

36 Performance

I. Obligations of seller and buyer.

   A. Seller to deliver or ship goods and buyer to pay for and accept them.

   B. Concurrent conditions, satisfied by tender.

   C. Sales contract fixes obligations; UCC provides rules for construction of contract and fills in open terms.

II. Delivery or shipment.

   A. Tender of goods.
      1. Entitles seller to payment and acceptance by buyer.
      2. Consists of:
         a. Putting and holding conforming goods at buyer's disposition and
         b. Giving buyer notification necessary to enable him or her to take delivery.
      3. Must be at a reasonable hour and kept available for a reasonable period.
      4. Must be at seller's place of business, or, if none, at seller's residence, except where parties know goods are located at some other place, then at that place. Parties may agree otherwise.

   B. Shipment of the goods. Seller's duty is to:
      1. Put conforming goods in possession of shipper and make appropriate shipping contract.
      2. Obtain and tender document to enable buyer to pick up goods.
      3. Notify buyer.

   C. Improper delivery. If goods do not conform to the contract, buyer may:
      1. Reject all of the goods or
      2. Accept all of the goods or
      3. Accept any commercial units of the goods and reject the rest.

   D. Cure of nonconforming tender or delivery. Seller may cure:

       1.   By timely notice of intention to cure and delivery of conforming goods within contract time.

       2.   By timely notice and substituting conforming goods within reasonable time after contract time where seller had reasonable grounds to believe non-conforming goods would be accepted with or without money allowance.

  E. Delay or nondelivery.

       1.   Constitutes breach of contract.

       2.   Excused where performance becomes impractical due to either:

          a.   An event occurring in conflict with basic assumption of contract or

          b.   Compliance with governmental regulation.

          c.   Seller must allocate production if event affects only part of production capacity.

III.   Payment.

  A. Tender.

       1.   A condition of seller's duty to tender delivery.

       2.   By check.

          a.   Conditional payment, defeated by dishonor.

          b.   Seller may demand cash but then must give reasonable time for buyer to get it.

  B. Right of inspection.

       1.   Buyer has right of inspection before payment except where sales contract provides for:

          a.   COD shipment, or

          b.   Payment against document of title.

       2.   Time, place, and method of inspection are entirely independent of time and place:

          a.   Where identification occurs,

          b.   Where risk of loss passes, or

          c.   Where seller is obligated to make delivery.

       3.   Expenses of inspection are borne by buyer but may be recovered from seller if goods are nonconforming.

       4.   Where payment is required prior to inspection, it:

          a.   Does not constitute acceptance of goods.

          b.   Does not impair buyer's right to inspect and reject.

IV.   Acceptance of non-conforming goods.

  A. Buyer has three alternatives—to accept, reject, or revoke acceptance of goods.

  B. Buyer must pay contract rate for any goods accepted.

C. Acceptance occurs when:
 1. After opportunity to inspect and despite nonconformity, buyer:
  a. Indicates to seller that they are conforming or that he or she will take or retain them.
  b. Fails to make an effective rejection.
 2. Buyer does any act inconsistent with seller's ownership.

V. Rejection of goods.

 A. Must notify seller within reasonable time.
 B. If nonmerchant buyer, only duty is to hold goods a reasonable time.
 C. If merchant buyer, must:
  1. Follow reasonable instructions.
  2. Make reasonable effort to resell if goods are perishable or likely to decline in value rapidly.
 D. Buyer may recover damages for nondelivery.
 E. Cannot reject accepted goods.

VI. Revocation of acceptance of goods.

 A. Buyer must have accepted:
  1. On assumption that nonconformity would be cured and it was not or
  2. Without discovery of nonconformity if acceptance was induced either:
   a. By the difficulty of discovery of the nonconformity or
   b. By the seller's assurance.
 B. Revocation must be in reasonable time.
 C. Buyer has same rights and duties as if he or she had rejected the goods.

VII. Adequate assurances of performance.

 A. Parties have right to be free from worry, to have sense of reliance that promised performance will be forthcoming.
 B. When one of the parties has reasonable grounds for insecurity with respect to the performance of the other, that party may in writing demand adequate assurance of due performance.
  1. Grounds may be:
   a. Failure of performance of other transactions or contracts.

      b.   Excessive use of credit.

      c.   Rumors and reputation.

  2.   Adequate assurance may vary from reaffirmation of intent to perform to posting of bond.

  3.   Between merchants, reasonableness of grounds for insecurity and adequacy of assurance is determined according to commercial standards.

C. Until assurance is received, party demanding assurance may suspend performance if commercially reasonable.

D. Failure to provide assurance within thirty days of receipt of demand is repudiation of contract.

E. Right to demand assurance is not barred by acceptance of an improper delivery or payment.

37 Remedies

I. Remedies of seller.
   A. Insolvency of buyer before goods are delivered.
      1. Seller may refuse to deliver except for cash, including payment for goods previously delivered under the contract.
      2. Right of stoppage in transit. Continues during transit until:
         a. Receipt of goods by buyer.
         b. Acknowledgment to buyer by any bailee except a carrier that he or she holds goods for buyer.
         c. Acknowledgment to buyer by carrier to reship or to act as warehouseman.
         d. Negotiation to buyer of negotiable document of title.
   B. Insolvency of buyer after goods are delivered.
      1. Seller may reclaim goods upon demand made within ten days after receipt.
      2. If buyer has made written misrepresentations of solvency within three months before delivery, seller may reclaim the goods at any time.
      3. Right to reclaim is subject to rights of good faith purchasers and lienors of the buyer.
   C. Breach by buyer.
      1. Nature of breaches.
         a. Wrongful rejection or revocation of acceptance of non-conforming goods.
         b. Failure to make payment due on or before delivery.
         c. Repudiation.
      2. Rights and remedies of seller.
         a. Identify conforming goods to the contract not already identified.
         b. Finish goods to avoid loss, or cease manufacture, and resell for scrap or salvage value.

156

  c. Stop goods in transit and withhold delivery.

  d. Cancel and recover damages.

 D. Right of resale.

  1. Seller may recover from buyer difference between resale price and contract price and incidental damages less expenses saved by buyer's breach.

  2. Resale may be at public or private sale.

   a. If private sale, buyer must have reasonable notice of seller's intention to resell.

   b. Purchaser takes goods free from any rights of original buyer even though seller may have failed to comply with UCC.

   c. Seller is not accountable for any profit made on resale.

 E. Measure of damages.

  1. Generally, the difference between the contract price and the market price.

  2. If the difference will not make the seller whole, the formula for damages is profit, reasonable overhead, incidental damages, and costs incurred less proceeds of resale.

  3. An action for the contract price may be maintained:

   a. Where goods were accepted by buyer or were lost or destroyed after risk of loss passed to buyer.

   b. Where goods were identified and seller has been unable to resell them and holds them for the buyer.

II. Remedies of buyer.

 A. Insolvency of seller.

  1. Buyer who has paid part or all of the price may recover identified goods even though they have not been shipped if seller becomes insolvent within ten days after receipt of first installment of the price and buyer tenders remainder of purchase price.

  2. If identification has been made by buyer, he or she has right to recover goods only if they conform to contract.

 B. Seller's failure to deliver or repudiation. Buyer may:

  1. Cancel.

   a. Recover as much of the price as had been paid.

   b. "Cover" and have damages. *Cover* is the purchase of substitute goods; *Damages* is the difference in cost of cover and contract price plus or minus expenses incurred or saved.

  2. Recover the goods if they have been identified.

    a. Obtain decree of specific performance where goods are unique (compel performance).

    b. Obtain judgment of replevin where either cover cannot be effected or goods were shipped under reservation and satisfaction of security interest has been made or tendered (obtain possession).

  C. Seller's delivery of nonconforming goods rightfully rejected or acceptance justifiably revoked by buyer. Buyer may:

    1. Cancel and recover as much of the price as has been paid.

    2. Cover and have damages.

    3. Resell but must account for profit.

III. Anticipatory repudiation.

  A. If either party repudiates contract so that its value is substantially impaired, other party may:

    1. Urge retraction and await performance for commercially reasonable time or

    2. Resort to remedy.

    3. Suspend own performance or

    4. Exercise seller's right to identify goods to contract or salvage unfinished goods.

  B. Retraction.

    1. Repudiating party may retract before next performance is due unless other party:

      a. Cancelled,

      b. Materially changed position, or

      c. Elected to treat repudiation as final.

    2. Must include assurance justifiably demanded.

    3. Reinstates repudiating party's rights with due allowance for delay caused other party.

IV. Installment contracts.

  A. Refers to contracts for delivery of goods in installments.

  B. Buyer may reject nonconforming installments, unless adequate assurance of cure is given, where nonconformity:

    1. Impairs value of installment and cannot be cured.

    2. Consists of defect in required documents.

  C. Where value of whole contract is impaired by nonconforming installment:

    1. Buyer may resort to appropriate remedies for breach of whole contract where contract was not reinstated by buyer's action.

    2. Buyer reinstates contract where he or she:

      a. Accepts nonconforming installment without notification to seller that contract is cancelled.

      b. Brings action only in regard to past installments.

      c. Demands performance of future installments.

V. Liquidated damages.

  A. The parties may provide for liquidated damages in their contract as long as the provision is reasonable.

  B. Where there is no provision for liquidated damages and the buyer defaults after paying part of the price, he or she can recover back:

     1. What has been paid less

     2. The smaller of either 20 percent of the total contract price or $500.

     3. The seller can offset against this amount any other damages as provided in the UCC.

VI. Modification or limitation of UCC remedies and damages. Sales contract may:

  A. Provide remedies in addition to or in substitution for UCC remedies.

  B. Provide exclusive remedy.

     1. Sole remedy for breach.

     2. If it fails its purpose, UCC remedies may be resorted to.

  C. Limit or alter damages recoverable under the UCC.

  D. Limit or exclude consequential damages unless unconscionable. Limitation of damages for personal injuries is *prima facie* unconscionable in consumer sales.

VII. Statute of limitations.

  A. Four years, except as varied when adopted by the states.

  B. Parties may agree to reduce period to not less than one year.

38 Warranties and Products Liability

I. Theories of actions for products liability.

    A. Breach of warranty.
        1. An express or implied undertaking of the seller.
        2. Action based on contract. Buyer has right to money judgment for breach.

    B. Common law negligence. Ordinary care required of seller.

    C. Strict liability in tort: Putting defective and dangerous articles on market constitutes a civil wrong.

II. Express warranties.

    A. Affirmation of fact or promise relating to the goods.
        1. Must be a part of the basis of the bargain.
            a. Question of fact for court or jury as to whether buyer relied on statement in deciding to contract with seller.
            b. If relied upon, is actionable whether made in preliminary negotiations (inducing purchase) or contemporaneously with sale.
            c. Seller may be bound by warranties made after sale, even without consideration.
        2. Need not be formal.
            a. Proof that words *warranty* or *guaranty* were used is not necessary to establish seller's liability.
            b. Buyer not required to establish that seller intended a warranty.
            c. May be oral or written, depending on requirements imposed on sale by Statute of Frauds.
        3. Warranties are not created by:
            a. Affirmations of the value of the goods.
            b. Statements of seller's opinion or commendation of the goods (puffing).
        4. Failure of goods to conform to affirmation or promise constitutes breach of warranty.

    B. Descriptions.
        1. Must be a part of the basis of the bargain.

          a. Applies where goods are sold by description.

          b. Need not be words. May be technical specifications or blueprints. Past deliveries may set implied description as to quality.

          c. Buyer must have relied on description.

          d. No reliance where buyer selects goods.

    2. Warranty is that goods shall conform to description.

C. Samples or models.

    1. Must be a part of the basis of the bargain.

          a. Applies where goods are sold by sample or model.

          b. Mere exhibition of sample does not establish warranty as to bulk. Actions of seller with reference to sample or fact that it was drawn from bulk must be established.

          c. If sample is processed goods, it does not constitute warranty as to nature of raw materials being sold.

          d. Model offered when goods are not at hand. Not treated as literal description. Warranty weakened where buyer asks for modifications.

    2. Buyer must have relied on sample or model.

    3. Warranty is that goods will conform.

III. Implied warranties.

A. Merchantability.

    1. Applies if seller is a merchant with respect to goods of the kind involved in the sales contract.

    2. To be merchantable the goods must at least:

          a. Pass without objection in the trade. Be resalable in the normal course of business. Be of fair average quality, if fungible goods. Price is an index of intended quality.

          b. Be fit for the ordinary purpose for which such goods are used.

          c. Run, within variations permitted by the agreement, of even kind, quality, and quantity within each unit and among all units involved.

          d. Be adequately contained, packaged, and labeled, as per agreement.

          e. Conform to labeling.

    3. Warranty applies to food and drink served on premises.

    4. Goods sold by brand name must have average quality of that brand.

B. Fitness for particular purpose.

    1. Applies if:

       a.   Seller has reason to know purpose for which goods are required.

       b.   Buyer is relying on seller's skill or judgment in selecting suitable goods.

   2.   Purpose may be unusual or extraordinary.

C. Other implied warranties may arise from usages of trade.

IV.   Exclusion or modification of implied warranties.

   A. Merchantability. To exclude or modify:
       1.   Language must mention merchantability.
       2.   In case of a writing, must be conspicuous.

   B. Fitness warranty. To exclude or modify:
       1.   Must be by a writing and conspicuous.
       2.   Sufficient language: "There are no warranties which extend beyond the description on the face hereof."

   C. All implied warranties are excluded by expressions "as is," "with all faults," or similar language.

   D. An implied warranty may be excluded or modified by course of dealing, course of performance, or usage of trade.

   E. Buyer's inspection or refusal to inspect prior to sale excludes implied warranty as to defects that ought to have been discovered thereby.

V.   Privity and third party beneficiaries.

   A. Plaintiff must establish privity of contract in breach of warranty action. If defendant is a retailer, he or she may implead wholesaler and/or manufacturer.

   B. Limited third party beneficiary rights provided by UCC.
       1.   Suit permitted for breach of express or implied warranty by any natural person who:
          a.   Is a member of the family or household or a guest in the home of the buyer,
          b.   May be reasonably expected to consume or be affected by the goods, and
          c.   Is injured in person by the breach of warranty.
       2.   Seller may not exclude or limit third party rights provided in the UCC.

VI.   Common law negligence.

   A. Manufacturer has duty to members of the public to exercise ordinary care.
       1.   Applies to manufacturing, inspecting, and testing product.

2. Degree of care exercised is measured against standards of the industry. Care below standards is negligence.

3. Violation of statutory standards is negligence per se. In such cases, industry standards are immaterial.

4. Must give warning if manufacturer had or ought to have had knowledge of any inherent dangers.

B. *Res ipsa loquitur* (the thing speaks for itself).

   1. Doctrine applies where:

      a. Accident is type which generally results through negligence.

      b. Defendant has exclusive control of factors causing injury.

      c. Plaintiff proves no intervening negligence.

   2. Rebuttable presumption of negligence. Defendant has burden of removing all questions of negligence on its part.

C. Retailer has duty of ordinary care but is not required to inspect sealed cartons unless suspect.

D. Privity not necessary.

E. Failure of injured party to use ordinary care (contributory negligence) and voluntary use, knowing of danger (assumption of risk), are defenses.

VII. Strict liability in tort.

A. Seller liable to ultimate user for defective and unreasonably dangerous products.

   1. Applies where:

      a. Seller is in business of selling such product.

      b. Defective product reaches user without substantial change.

B. Differs from common law negligence in that degree of care used by seller is not an issue in the case and contributory negligence of user is not a defense.

C. Differs from implied warranty theory in that seller cannot use defenses of lack of timely notice of breach, disclaimer, and lack of privity.

D. Elements of strict liability.

   1. Defect.

      a. Dangerous design.

      b. Lack of safety devices.

      c. Unsafe materials.

      d. Lack of warning.

   2. Unreasonably dangerous.

      a. Ordinary person would not expect danger from ordinary use.

  b. Product incapable of being made safe for ordinary use.
  3. Defective when it left seller.
E. Defenses.
  1. Product altered.
  2. Product used knowingly for improper purpose or in improper manner.
  3. Product used with knowledge of defect and of full extent of danger (assumption of risk defense).

VIII. Other warranties.

A. Warranty of title.
  1. Nature of warranty.
    a. Good title.
    b. Rightful transfer.
    c. Free from security interests, liens, or encumbrances of which buyer has no knowledge.
  2. Applies to all sales and may be excluded or modified only:
    a. By specific language, or
    b. If buyer has reason to know seller does not claim title in himself or herself, or
    c. If seller is purporting to sell only such right or title as seller or third person may have.
B. Warranty against infringement.
  1. Seller's warranty.
    a. Applies to merchants regularly dealing in goods of the same kind.
    b. Seller warrants goods shall be delivered free from rightful claims of third persons by way of infringement.
  2. Buyer's warranty.
    a. Arises where buyer furnishes specifications.
    b. Must hold seller harmless against claims arising out of compliance with specifications.

IX. Magnuson-Moss Warranty Act.

A. Federal law to prevent deceptive warranty practices.
B. Applicable only to consumer sales.
C. Applicable only if seller elects to make an express written warranty relating to:
  1. The quality or performance of the product, or
  2. An undertaking to refund, repair, replace or take other action with respect to the product.

D. It has no effect on implied warranties, except that it prohibits a disclaimer of an implied warranty if:
1. An express written warranty is given, or
2. Within ninety days after the sale, a service contract is
made with the consumer.

PART NINE
Commercial Paper
and Secured Transactions

Introduction to
Commercial Paper

I. Promissory notes, drafts, and checks are the principal kinds of instruments by which business is normally financed.

    A. To qualify as commercial paper, an instrument must be signed by the maker or drawer and contain an unconditional promise or order to pay to order or bearer a sum certain in money on demand or at a definite time.

    B. Uniform Commercial Code, Article 3, Commercial Paper, and Article 4, Bank Deposits and Collections, as modified and adopted by state legislatures and interpreted by state courts, is applicable law.

II. Types of commercial paper.

    A. Notes: Two party paper.
        1. Maker: One promising to pay a stated sum of money at a particular time to the order of the payee.
        2. Payee: One to receive the sum of money from the maker.

    B. Types of notes.
        1. Collateral notes: Secured by personal property.
        2. Installment notes: Principal sum payable in installments.
        3. Real estate mortgage notes: Secured by a mortgage on real property.
        4. Certificates of deposit: Notes issued by bank acknowledging receipt of money and promising to repay it upon terms stated.

    C. Drafts (bills of exchange): Three-party paper.
        1. Drawer: One ordering drawee to pay a sum of money.
        2. Drawee: One ordered to pay a sum of money to the payee.
        3. Payee: One to receive the sum of money from the drawee.

    D. Types of drafts.
        1. Time draft: Payable at a future date.

167

2. Sight draft: Payable immediately upon presentation to the drawee.
3. Trade acceptance: Time draft used in the sale of goods.
4. Bank draft: Drawer and drawee are banks.
5. Checks: Drawee is a bank; instrument payable on demand.

III. Formal requisites of commercial paper.

A. The instrument must be in writing and signed by the maker of a note or the drawer of a draft.
1. No particular form or type of writing is required.
2. Anything adopted at the time for a signature stands as such.
3. Parol evidence is admissible to identify the signer. When signer is identified, the signature is effective.

B. A note must contain a promise to pay and draft must contain an order to pay.
1. A promise is an undertaking to pay and must be more than the acknowledgment of an obligation. An IOU, for example, is not a promise.
2. An order is a direction to pay and must be more than an authorization or request, and it must identify the person to pay with reasonable certainty. Words of courtesy will not convert the direction to a mere request.

C. The promise or order must be unconditional, without reservation or contingency.
1. Statements that make the instrument conditional.
a. That it is subject to or governed by any other agreement.
b. That it is to be paid only out of a particular fund or source, unless:
(1) The instrument is issued by a government or governmental agency or unit or
(2) The instrument is limited to payment out of the entire assets of a partnership, unincorporated association, trust, or estate which issued the instrument.
2. Statements that will not make the instrument conditional.
a. That it states the transaction which gave rise to the instrument.
b. That it refers to or states that it arises out of a separate agreement or refers to a separate agreement

for rights as to prepayment or acceleration.

c. That it states it is secured, whether by mortgage, reservation of title, or otherwise.

d. That it indicates a particular account to be charged or any other fund or source from which reimbursement is expected.

D. The instrument must be payable *to order* or *to bearer* —words of negotiability.

1. Order paper: an instrument payable either to the order of any person, or to any person or his or her order, an instrument payable to the assigns of any person, and an instrument on the face of which, "exchange" or the like is conspicuously designated and a payee is named. The following are proper payees:

a. Two or more payees together (Jane Doe *and* Richard Roe) or in the alternative (Jane Doe *or* Richard Roe).

b. An estate, trust, or fund, in which case it is payable to the order of the representative of such estate, trust, or fund or the representative's successors.

c. An office or an officer by title as such, in which case it is payable to the principal, but the incumbent of the office or successors may act as if they were the holders.

d. A partnership or unincorporated association, in which case it is payable to the partnership or association and may be indorsed or transferred by any person authorized to do so.

2. Bearer paper: An instrument payable to:

a. Bearer or the order of bearer.

b. A specified person or bearer.

c. Cash or the order of cash, or any other indication which does not purport to designate a specific payee.

E. The sum payable in money must be certain.

1. "Money" means a medium of exchange authorized or adopted by a domestic or foreign government as a part of its currency.

2. It is a sum certain even though it is to be paid:

a. With stated interest or by stated installments.

b. With stated different rates of interest before and after default or before and after a specified date.

3. If acts are required in addition to payment of money, the instrument is nonnegotiable unless such acts are connected with the payment of money or provide security therefore, such as the following:

    a. A promise or power to maintain, protect, or increase collateral.

    b. A power to sell collateral in case of default in payment of principal or interest on the instrument.

    c. A term authorizing confession of judgment on the instrument if it is not paid when due.

    d. A term purporting to waive the benefit of any law intended for the advantage or protection of any obligor.

    e. A term in a draft providing that the payee, by indorsing or cashing it, acknowledges full satisfaction of an obligation of the drawer.

    f. A promise to pay collection or attorney's fees.

F. The instrument must be payable on demand or at a definite time.

    1. Demand paper: Instruments payable on demand, on presentation, at sight, and those in which no time for payment is stated—such as a check—are all payable on demand.

    2. Time paper: Instruments payable at a definite time other than on demand. The following terms are considered a definite time:

        a. On or before a stated date or at a fixed period after a stated date.

        b. At a fixed period after sight.

        c. At a definite time subject to any acceleration.

        d. At a definite time subject to extension at the option of the holder. However, the holder cannot exercise this option if the maker or acceptor tenders full payment when the instrument is due.

        e. At a definite time subject to extension to a further definite time at the option of the maker or acceptor or automatically upon or after a specified act or event.

    3. An instrument which is payable only upon an act or event uncertain as to time of occurrence is not payable at a definite time even though the act or event has occurred. Therefore, it is not negotiable.

G. In the case of a draft, the drawee must be described so that he or she may be readily identified.

H. If an instrument does not comply with the above requirements, it still may be legal, transferable, and enforceable as a simple contract.

IV.   Nonessentials of negotiability.

   A.   For value received.
   B.   Place made or drawn or place payable.
   C.   Presence or absence of a seal.
   D.   A date.
   1.   If undated, date of issuance is true date.
   2.   If wrong date is inserted, stated date is true date in hands of a holder in due course.
   3.   If antedated or postdated, the time when it is payable is determined by the stated date if the instrument is payable on demand or at a fixed period after date.
   E.   An incomplete instrument cannot be enforced until completed, but when it is completed in accordance with authority given, it is effective as completed. If the completion is unauthorized, it is unenforceable except in the hands of a holder in due course.

V.   Rules of construction.

   A.   Handwritten terms control typewritten and printed terms, and typewritten control printed.
   B.   An instrument made payable both to order and to bearer is payable to order unless the bearer words are handwritten or typewritten.
   C.   Words control figures except that if the words are ambiguous, figures control.
   D.   Unless otherwise specified, a provision for interest means interest at the judgment rate at the place of payment from the date of the instrument, or if it is undated, from the date of issue.

40 Transfer and Negotiation

I. Rights acquired by a transfer, either by assignment or negotiation.

A. Shelter provision: Transferee obtains whatever rights the transferor had. However, the transferee cannot improve his or her position by taking from a later holder in due course if:
1. The transferee has been a party to any fraud or illegality affecting the instrument or
2. The transferee as a prior holder had notice of a defense or claim against the instrument.

B. Any transfer for value of an instrument not then payable to bearer gives the transferee the right to have the unqualified indorsement of the transferor. Negotiation takes effect only when the indorsement is made.

II. Negotiation.

A. Negotiation is the transfer of an instrument in such form that the transferee becomes a holder.
1. Holder is a person who is in possession of an instrument drawn, issued, or indorsed to him or her or to his or her order or to bearer or in blank.
2. If instrument is payable to bearer, it is negotiated by delivery.
3. If instrument is payable to order, it is negotiated by delivery and necessary indorsement.
4. Delivery means the transfer of the actual or constructive possession of the instrument from one person to another.
5. When an indorsement is necessary, negotiation takes effect only when the indorsement is made, and until that time there is no presumption that the transferee is the owner.

B. Indorsements—how made.
1. Must be written by or on behalf of the holder and on

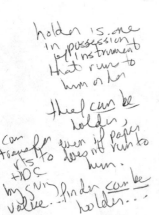

holder is one in possession of Instrument that runs to him or her

thief can be holder, Can transfer rts to even if paper doesn't run to him. +HDC in SW) finder can be value. holder...

172

the instrument or on a paper so firmly affixed thereto as to become a part of the instrument.

2. Must convey the entire instrument. If it purports to be less than the entire instrument it operates only as a partial assignment.

3. Words of assignment, condition, waiver, guaranty, limitation, or disclaimer of liability and the like accompanying an indorsement do not affect its character as an indorsement.

4. Where an instrument is made payable to a person under a misspelled name or one other than his or her own, such as a trade name, the person may indorse in that name or his or her own or both. The person taking the instrument can require indorsement of both names.

5. Indorsements do not need words of negotiability as the face of the instrument does.

III. Types of indorsements.

A. Special: Specifies the indorsee. May not be further negotiated without indorsee's signature.

B. Blank: Does not specify indorsee. May consist of indorser's signature only. Makes instrument bearer paper.

1. The holder can convert the blank indorsement to a special indorsement by writing over the signature of the indorser any contract consistent with the character of the indorsement.

2. Subsequent special indorsement revives order character of instrument.

C. Restrictive—four types:

1. Conditional: The indorser makes the rights of the indorsee and any subsequent holder subject to the happening of a certain event.

2. Purports to prohibit further transfer, such as "Pay A only." This is given the same effect as an unrestricted indorsement.

3. For deposit or collection: Prohibits any further use of the instrument other than to deposit it in the indorser's account.

4. In trust: Only the first taker under this indorsement must see to it that the money he or she expended was applied consistently with the indorsement.

D. Qualified (without recourse).

1. Passes full title to the instrument.

2. The indorser does not have liability conditioned upon due presentment, dishonor, and notice but still has warranty liability.

IV. Duty of banks in the case of restricted indorsements.

A. A depository bank must honor restrictive indorsements as provided above.
B. An intermediary bank, or a payor bank which is not the depository bank, need concern itself only with the indorsement of its immediate transferor and may disregard any other restrictive indorsements.

V. Reacquisition of an instrument.

A. If a prior party reacquires an instrument, any intervening party is discharged as against the reacquiring party and any subsequent holders not in due course.
B. The reacquiring party may cancel any intervening indorsement before further negotiation. Then intervening indorser and subsequent indorsers prior to reacquiring party are discharged as against any subsequent holders.

VI. An indorsement by any person in the name of a named payee is effective if:

A. An imposter by use of the mails or otherwise has induced the maker or drawer to issue the instrument to him or her or a confederate in the name of the payee or
B. A person signing as or on behalf of a maker or drawer intends the payee to have no interest in the instrument or
C. An agent or employee of the maker or drawer has supplied him or her with the name of the payee, intending the latter to have no such interest.

VII. Negotiation subject to rescission.

A. A negotiation is effective even though:
1. It is made by a minor, a corporation exceeding its powers, or any other person without capacity.
2. It is obtained by fraud, duress, or mistake of any kind.
3. It is part of an illegal transaction.
4. It is made in breach of duty.
B. Such negotiation is subject to rescission or any other remedy permitted by law except as against a subsequent holder in due course.

41

I. A holder in due course is one who holds under such circumstances as make his or her rights against prior parties superior to those of former owners.

II. To be a holder in due course, one must be a holder for value, in good faith, and without notice that it is overdue or has been dishonored or that any person has a defense against it or a claim to it.

A. Requirement of value.
1. A holder takes for value only to the extent that the agreed consideration has been performed.
2. A purchaser of a limited interest can be a holder in due course only to the extent of the interest purchased (e.g., security interest).
3. Value also consists of a past or antecedent debt whether or not due.
4. Giving another negotiable instrument is present value.
5. A bank is deemed to have paid value on instruments deposited in customers' accounts on a FIFO basis of withdrawals by the customers.

B. Requirement of good faith.
1. Means lack of actual knowledge of a defense.
2. Honesty in fact in the conduct or transaction concerned.

C. Without notice requirement.
1. A person has notice of a fact when he or she:
a. Has actual knowledge of it or
b. Has received notice or notification of it or
c. From all the facts and circumstances known to him or her at the time in question, has reason to know that it exists.
2. Notice instrument is overdue.
a. When the purchaser has reason to know that any part of the principal amount is overdue or that

175

there is an uncured default in payment of another instrument of the same series.

   b. When the purchaser has reason to know that acceleration of the instrument has been made.

   c. When the purchaser has reason to know that he or she is taking a demand instrument after demand has been made or more than a reasonable length of time after its issuance.

     (1) What is a reasonable time depends upon the facts of the particular case, business custom, etc.

     (2) A reasonable time for a check is presumed to be thirty days.

3. Notice instrument has been dishonored: Refusal of a party to pay or accept it.

4. Notice of claim or defense.

   a. The purchaser has notice if the instrument is so incomplete, bears such visible evidence of forgery or alteration, or is otherwise so irregular as to call into question its validity, terms, or ownership or to create an ambiguity as to the party to pay.

   b. The purchaser has notice if he or she knows that the obligation of any party is voidable in whole or in part, or that all parties have been discharged.

   c. The purchaser has notice of a claim against the instrument when he or she has knowledge that a fiduciary has negotiated the instrument in payment of or as security for his or her own debt or in any transaction for his or her own benefit or otherwise in breach of duty.

5. Knowledge of the following facts does not of itself give the purchaser notice of a defense or claim:

   a. That the instrument is antedated or postdated;

   b. That the instrument was originally issued or negotiated for an executory promise or was accompanied by a separate agreement, unless the purchaser knows that the promise has not been kept;

   c. That any party has signed as an accommodation.

   d. That an incomplete instrument has been completed, unless the purchaser has notice of the fact that the completion was improper;

   e. That any person negotiating the instrument is or was a fiduciary;

       f.   That there has been default in payment of interest on the instrument or in payment of any other instrument, except one of the same series.

  D. A payee may be a holder in due course.

III.   Defenses available against a holder in due course: Real defenses.

  A. Minority.
     1. A defense to the extent that it is a defense to a simple contract under the laws of the state involved.
     2. The only defense good against a holder in due course based on voidability of a contract. All other defenses hereinafter discussed render the instrument absolutely void.

  B. Incapacity (other than minority), duress, and illegality of the transaction, to the extent the obligation is rendered void under the law of the state involved. Examples are:
     1. In most states, the contracts of a person who has been adjudicated insane are absolutely void.
     2. Duress to a very high degree. Degree varies from state to state.
     3. Illegality under state law: State statutes make certain transactions absolutely void, such as, contracts made pursuant to gambling transactions. If contract is only voidable, not a valid defense against a holder in due course.

  C. Fraud in the execution, but not fraud in the inducement.

  D. Discharge in bankruptcy.

  E. Any unauthorized or forged signature is wholly inoperative as that of the person whose name is signed unless he or she ratifies it or is precluded from denying it.

  F. Material alteration.
     1. Any alteration of an instrument is material which changes the contract of any party thereto in any respect, including any such change in:
        a. The number or relations of the parties.
        b. An incomplete instrument, by completing it otherwise than as authorized.
        c. The writing as signed, by adding to it or by removing any part of it.
     2. As against any person other than a subsequent holder in due course:
        a. Alteration by the holder which is both fraudulent and material discharges any party whose contract

is thereby changed unless that party assents or is precluded from asserting the defense.

    b.   No other alteration discharges any party and the instrument may be enforced according to its original tenor, or as to incomplete instruments, according to the authority given.

  3.   A subsequent holder in due course of an altered instrument can enforce it according to its original terms and, when an incomplete instrument has been completed, may enforce it as completed.

  4.   Any person who by negligence substantially contributes to a material alteration of the instrument or to the making of an unauthorized signature is precluded from asserting the alteration or lack of authority against a holder in due course.

G. Statute of limitations.

H. Defenses to a simple contract that are not included above are called personal defenses. Personal defenses are available against anyone but a holder in due course.

IV. Rights of a holder through a holder in due course (shelter provision).

  A. Even though one cannot qualify as a holder in due course, a person may have the rights of a holder in due course if a prior party qualified.

  B. Exception: The transferee who has been a party to any fraud or illegality affecting the instrument or who as a prior holder had notice of a defense or claim against it cannot improve his or her position by taking from a later holder in due course.

V. Consumer credit transactions.

  A. Many states have enacted statutes either abolishing or at least modifying the holder in due course statutes where commercial paper is issued in connection with a consumer credit transaction.

  B. Federal Trade Commission rule requires that any consumer credit contract (including commercial paper) contain a conspicuous notice stating that any holder of the contract takes it subject to all claims and defenses the debtor could assert against the seller.

Liability 42
of Parties

I. Liability based on signature.

  A. No person is liable on an instrument unless his or her signature appears thereon. However, the person may have warranty liability. (See Part IV)

  B. Liability of an agent.

    1. Agent personally liable if the instrument neither names the person represented nor shows that the agent signed in a representative capacity.

    2. Except as to the payee who knew of the agency, agent personally liable if:

      a. The instrument names the person represented but does not show that the agent signed in a representative capacity or

      b. If the instrument does not name the person represented but does show that the agent signed in a representative capacity.

    3. Any unauthorized signature operates as the signature of the unauthorized signer in favor of any person who in good faith pays the instrument and takes it for value.

II. Liability of primary parties (maker of a note, acceptor of a draft).

  A. Maker's contract.

    1. That he or she will pay the instrument according to its tenor at the time of the promise.

    2. Admits the existence of the payee and that person's then capacity to indorse.

  B. Acceptor's contract.

    1. Same as maker's contract above.

    2. Acceptance is the drawee's signed engagement to honor the draft as presented. It must be written on the draft and may consist of drawee's signature alone.

    3. Certification of a check is acceptance.

179

        a. Where a holder procures certification, the drawer and all prior indorsers are discharged.

        b. A bank has no obligation to certify a check.

    4. Acceptance varying draft.

        a. Where the drawee's acceptance in any manner varies the draft as presented, the holder may refuse the acceptance and treat the draft as dishonored.

        b. Where the holder assents to an acceptance varying the terms of the draft, each drawer and indorser who does not affirmatively assent is discharged.

C. Liability of primary parties for interest.

    1. Any party making tender of full payment to a holder when or after it is due is discharged to the extent of all subsequent liability for interest, costs, and attorney's fees.

    2. If a note or draft is payable at a special place (domiciled paper) and the maker or acceptor is able and ready to pay at that place when the instrument is due, it is equivalent to tender.

    3. If domiciled paper is payable at a bank in which the primary party has sufficient funds to pay the instrument and presentment by the holder is delayed without excuse beyond the time it is due, the risk of the solvency of the bank is assumed by the holder.

III. Liability of secondary parties (drawer of a draft, indorsers).

A. Secondary parties are conditionally liable in that there are certain conditions precedent before they can be held liable, namely, presentment, notice of dishonor, and, in some situations, protest.

    1. Contract of the drawer.

        a. The drawer agrees that upon dishonor of the draft and any necessary notice of dishonor or protest, he or she will pay the amount of the draft to the holder or to any indorser who takes it up.

        b. The drawer may disclaim this liability by drawing without recourse.

    2. Contract of indorser.

        a. Every indorser agrees that upon dishonor and any necessary notice of dishonor and protest he or she will pay the instrument according to its tenor at the time of indorsement to the holder or to any subsequent indorser who takes it up.

        b. Each indorser may disclaim this liability by indorsing without recourse.

B. Presentment.
   1. Presentment is a demand for acceptance or payment made upon the maker, acceptor, drawee, or other payor by or on behalf of the holder.
   2. Time of presentment.
      a. If an instrument is payable on a specified date, it is due for presentment on that date.
      b. If an instrument is payable after sight it must either be presented for acceptance or negotiated within a reasonable time after date or issue, whichever is later.
      c. Where an instrument is accelerated, presentment for payment is due within a reasonable time after the acceleration.
      d. With respect to the liability of any secondary party, presentment for acceptance or payment of any other instrument is due within a reasonable time after such party becomes liable thereon.
      e. In the case of a check, a reasonable time is presumed to be:
         (1) With respect to the liability of the drawer, thirty days after date or issue, whichever is later; and
         (2) With respect to the liability of an indorser, seven days after indorsement.

C. Notice of dishonor.
   1. An instrument is dishonored when presentment has been made and acceptance or payment is refused.
   2. Subject to any necessary notice of dishonor and protest, the holder has upon dishonor an immediate right of recourse against the drawers and indorsers.
   3. Any necessary notice must be given by a bank before midnight on the next banking day following the banking day on which it receives notice of dishonor.
   4. Any necessary notice must be given by any other person before midnight of the third business day after dishonor or receipt of notice of dishonor.
   5. Notice may be given in any reasonable manner.
   6. Notice operates for the benefit of all parties who have rights on the instrument against the party notified.

D. Protest.
   1. A protest is a certificate of dishonor made under the hand and seal of a United States consul or vice consul or a notary public or other person authorized to certify dishonor by the law of the place where dishonor occurs.

    2. Only required where a draft is drawn or payable out-
side the United States.

  E. Presentment, notice, and protest can be waived, or there
may be a justifiable excuse existing for not meeting these
conditions.

  F. Contract of accommodation party.

    1. An accommodation party is one who signs the instru-
ment in any capacity for the purpose of lending his or
her name to another party to it.

    2. The accommodation party is liable in the capacity in
which he or she has signed even though the taker
knows of the accommodation.

  G. Contract of guarantor.

    1. The use of the words *payment guaranteed* by an
indorser or drawer makes the user primarily liable.

    2. The use of the words *collection guaranteed* waives pre-
sentment, notice, and protest but does not make the
user primarily liable. He or she cannot be held until the
holder has exhausted all remedies against the primary
party.

IV. Warranties on transfer.

  A. Any person who transfers an instrument and receives consideration warrants to the transferee and, if the transfer is
by indorsement, to any subsequent holder who takes the
instrument in good faith that:

    1. He or she has a good title to the instrument or is
authorized to obtain payment or acceptance on behalf
of one who has a good title and the transfer is otherwise rightful; and

    2. All signatures are genuine or authorized; and

    3. The instrument has not been materially altered; and

    4. No defense of any party is good against the transferor;
and

    5. He or she has no knowledge of any insolvency pro-
ceeding instituted with respect to the maker or acceptor or the drawer of an unaccepted instrument.

  B. By transferring without recourse the transferor limits the
obligation stated in Item 4 above to a warranty that he or
she has no knowledge of such a defense.

V. Warranties on presentment. Any person who obtains payment
or acceptance and any prior transferor warrants to a person
who in good faith pays or accepts that:

    A. He or she has a good title to the instrument or is authorized
to obtain payment or acceptance on behalf of one who has
a good title; and

    B. He or she has no knowledge that the signature of the maker
or drawer is unauthorized, except that this warranty is not
given by a holder in due course acting in good faith:

        1. To a maker with respect to the maker's own signature;
or

        2. To a drawer with respect to the drawer's own signature,
whether or not the drawer is also the drawee; or

        3. To an acceptor of a draft if the holder in due course
took the draft after the acceptance or obtained the acceptance without knowledge that the drawer's signature was unauthorized; and

    C. The instrument has not been materially altered, except
that this warranty is not given by a holder in due course
acting in good faith:

        1. To the maker of a note; or

        2. To the drawer of a draft, whether or not the drawer is
also the drawee; or

        3. To the acceptor of a draft with respect to an alteration
made prior to the acceptance, if the holder in due
course took the draft after the acceptance, even
though the acceptance provided *payable as originally
drawn* or equivalent terms; or

        4. To the acceptor of a draft with respect to an alteration
made after the acceptance.

VI. Liability for conversion.

    A. An instrument is converted when:

        1. A drawee to whom it is delivered for acceptance re-
fuses to return it on demand.

        2. Any person to whom it is delivered for payment refuses
on demand either to pay or to return it.

        3. It is paid on a forged indorsement.

    B. In an action in conversion against a drawee, the measure
of liability is the face amount of the instrument. In any
other action for conversion, the measure of liability is presumed to be the face amount of the instrument.

VII. Termination of liability.

    A. Payment or satisfaction.

        1. The liability of any party is discharged to the extent of
the party's payment or satisfaction to the holder.

    2. Only the liability of the paying party is discharged, and if there are others liable to him or her, the party may enforce the instrument against them.

B. Tender of payment.
    1. Any party making tender of full payment to a holder when or after it is due is discharged to the extent of all subsequent liability for interest, costs, and attorney's fees.
    2. The holder's refusal of such tender wholly discharges any party who has a right of recourse against the party making the tender.

C. Cancellation and renunciation.
    1. The holder of an instrument may without consideration discharge any party:
        a. In any manner apparent on the face of the instrument or the indorsement, as by intentionally canceling the instrument or the party's signature by destruction or mutilation or by striking out the party's signature; or
        b. By renouncing his or her rights in a writing, signed and delivered, or by surrender of the instrument to the party to be discharged.

D. Impairment of recourse or of collateral.
    1. The holder discharges any party to the instrument to the extent that without such party's consent the holder:
        a. Releases or agrees not to sue any person against whom such party, to the knowledge of the holder, has a right of recourse;
        b. Agrees to suspend the right to enforce the instrument or collateral against such person;
        c. Otherwise discharges such person; or
        d. Unjustifiably impairs any collateral given by or on behalf of the party or any person against whom such party has a right of recourse.
    2. By express reservation of rights against a party with a right of recourse the holder preserves:
        a. All rights against such party as of the time when the instrument was originally due; and
        b. The right of the party to pay the instrument as of that time; and
        c. All rights of such party to recourse against others.

E. Intervening parties are discharged upon reacquisition of an instrument by a prior holder.

F. Alteration by the holder which is both fraudulent and material discharges any party whose contract is thereby changed.

G. Where a holder of a check procures certification, the drawer and all prior indorsers are discharged.

H. Where the holder assents to an acceptance varying the terms of the draft, each drawer and indorser who does not affirmatively assent is discharged.

I. Any unexcused delay in presentment, notice of dishonor, or protest will discharge:

1. Any indorser, and

2. Any drawer to the extent that during the delay the drawee has funds available for payment but becomes insolvent during the delay, thereby depriving the drawer of the benefits of these funds to cover the instrument.

J. No discharge of any party is effective against a subsequent holder in due course unless the holder has notice thereof when he or she takes the instrument.

43 Checks and Banks

I. Checks and payment thereof.

    A. A check is a draft drawn on a bank and payable on demand.

        1. Negotiability is not affected by the fact that a check is undated, antedated, or postdated, and where it is antedated or postdated, time of payment is determined by the stated date.

        2. Payable out of deposit in checking account of customer when ordered to do so by the depositor issuing a check, but bank must pay only in accordance with the order.

        3. The bank may properly charge the customer's account even though an overdraft results.

        4. Good faith payment to a holder may be charged to customer's account only according to original tenor if check was altered, and if issued uncompleted, then in accordance with its completed tenor unless bank had notice the completion was improper.

    B. Bank's failure to pay check.

        1. Bank is liable to its customer for damages proximately caused by wrongful dishonor, and when the dishonor occurs through mistake the customer can only recover actual damages. Proximately caused damage may include damages for arrest and prosecution of the customer and consequential damages.

        2. Bank is not liable to pay the holder of a check unless it is certified, even though the drawer has sufficient funds on deposit.

        3. A bank has no obligation to pay a check more than six months after its date, unless certified, but it may pay such check and charge the drawer's account if acting in good faith.

    C. Stop payment order.

        1. A customer may order the bank not to pay a previously issued check, but such order must be received by the

bank in time to provide opportunity to comply.

2. An oral stop order is effective for fourteen days, and a written order for six months; the latter may be renewed in writing.

3. The burden of proving the loss resulting from payment contrary to the stop order is on the customer.

4. A customer may stop payment of a postdated check, and the bank will be liable thereon if it paid the check before its stated date.

5. If a payor bank has paid an item over a stop order of the drawer, in order to prevent unjust enrichment and to the extent necessary to prevent loss to the bank, the bank may be subrogated to the rights of:

   a. Any holder in due course of the item against the drawer or maker; and

   b. The payee or any other holder against the drawer or maker on the item or under the transaction that gave rise to it; and

   c. The drawer or maker against the payee or any other holder of the item with respect to the transaction out of which it arose.

D. Death or incompetence of customer.

1. A drawee or collecting bank has no authority to pay or collect an item if it knows of the adjudication of incompetence of the customer and has a reasonable opportunity to act on such knowledge.

2. After death of a customer the bank may continue to certify or pay checks for ten days unless ordered to stop payment by a person claiming an interest in the account.

II. Payment not as ordered.

A. Forged indorsements on checks result in the bank making payment wrongfully, and the amount of the check must be returned to the drawer's account. The bank may then seek recovery from either the forger or subsequent indorsers after the forgery.

B. When the drawee bank pays a raised check, but not in accordance with the order of the customer as drawn:

1. The bank must reimburse the customer's account.

2. The bank can recover from the person altering the check or indorsers after the alteration.

C. Customer's duty to discover and report unauthorized signature or alteration.

1. A customer must exercise reasonable care and prompt-

      ness is examining his or her bank statement to discover an unauthorized signature or any alteration and notify the bank promptly after discovery of irregularity.

2. If the bank has exercised ordinary care and suffers a loss because of the failure of the depositor to examine his or her statement and checks, the customer is precluded from asserting the unauthorized signature or the alteration against the bank.

3. The customer is also precluded from asserting against the bank an unauthorized signature or alteration by the same wrongdoer on any check paid in good faith by the bank after the first check and statement were available to the customer for a reasonable period, not exceeding fourteen days, and before the bank receives notification from the customer of any such unauthorized signature or alteration.

4. Without regard to lack of care of either the customer or the bank, the customer must discover and report an unauthorized signature or any alteration within one year after the statement is made available to him or her, and has three years from that time to discover and report any unauthorized indorsement.

III. Final payment.

    A. An item is finally paid by a payor bank when it has done any of the following:

1. Paid the item in cash or

2. Settled for the item without reserving the right to revoke, or

3. Completed the posting of the item to the account of the drawer or other person, to be charged or

4. Made a provisional settlement for the item and failed to revoke the same in the manner and time permitted.

    B. Stop order initiated after final payment is ineffective.

Secured Transactions

44

I. Uniform Commercial Code, Article 9, Secured Transactions, as modified and adopted by state legislatures and interpreted by state courts is applicable law.

II. Security interest attaches when there is:
   A. A security agreement.
   B. Value has been given.
   C. The debtor has rights in the collateral.

III. The security agreement.
   A. May be oral if collateral in possession of secured party; otherwise must be written and signed by debtor. In the case of personal property exempt from execution, it must be signed by debtor's spouse, except purchase money security interests.
   B. Must contain description of collateral. In the case of crops, gas, oil, minerals, and timber, must contain description of land.
   C. May provide that collateral, whenever acquired, shall secure all obligations covered by the security agreement, except consumer goods when given as additional security unless the debtor acquires rights in them within ten days after the secured party gives value.
   D. Obligations covered by a security agreement may include future advances or other value whether or not the advances or value is given pursuant to commitment.
   E. A security interest is not invalid or fraudulent by reason of liberty in the debtor to use, commingle, or dispose of all or part of the collateral; or to collect or compromise accounts, contract rights, or chattel paper; or to use, commingle, or dispose of proceeds; or by reason of the failure of the secured party to require the debtor to account for proceeds or to replace collateral.

IV.   Perfection of the security interest.

    A. The security interest is not effective against third parties or debtor's trustee in bankruptcy unless it is perfected.

    B. Filing is necessary to perfect all security interests except in cases of:
      1. Collateral in the possession of the secured party.
      2. Purchase money security interests in consumer goods other than fixtures and motor vehicles.
      3. Assignment of less than a significant part of outstanding accounts of assignor.

    C. Financing statement is the document that must be filed.

    D. A purchase money security interest is one given by the debtor/buyer in the goods purchased (collateral) to secure the loan used to pay part or all of the purchase price. Secured party may be the seller or a third party advancing the purchase price.

V.   Financing statement.

    A. Must contain names and addresses of debtor and secured party and must be signed by the debtor.

    B. Must contain statement indicating types or describing items of collateral. Any description is sufficient so long as it reasonably identifies the collateral.

    C. If covering crops or fixtures, must give description of real estate and name of record owner.

    D. Security agreement is sufficient as a financing statement if it conforms with above requirements.

    E. Financing statement may be filed before security agreement is made or before security interest attaches. In such case, security interest is perfected when it attaches.

VI.   Place of filing. Financing statements related to:

    A. Farm equipment, accounts, consumer goods: Register of deeds in county of debtor's residence.

    B. Crops and goods which are to become fixtures: Office where mortgage on real estate would be recorded.

    C. In other cases, office of Secretary of State and office of Register of Deeds in county of debtor's place of business or residence. (Dual filing.)

    D. A filed financing statement is effective for a period of five years from the date of filing.

    E. A continuation statement may be filed by the secured party within six months prior to the expiration of the five-year period mentioned in Part D above.

VII. Goods.

    A. Consumer goods: Goods used or bought for use primarily for personal, family, or household use.

        1. In the case of nonpurchase money financing, the financing statement must be filed locally.

        2. In the case of purchase money financing, no filing is required for perfection, but if the secured party does not file, a buyer will take free of the security interest if he or she buys without knowledge of it, for value, and for personal or household use.

    B. Equipment: Goods used or bought for use primarily in business, or if the goods are not included in definitions of inventory, farm products or consumer goods.

    C. Farm products: Crops, livestock, or supplies used or produced in farming operations, or products of crops or livestock in their unmanufactured states, and in the possession of a debtor engaged in raising, fattening, grazing, or other farming operations.

    D. Inventory: Goods held by a person for sale or lease, or to be furnished under contracts of service or, if he or she has so furnished them or if they are raw materials, work in process, or materials used or consumed in a business.

        1. A buyer in ordinary course of business takes free of the security interest in inventory even though it is perfected and the buyer knows of it, provided the buyer does not actually know that the sale violates the terms of the security agreement.

    E. Proceeds: Includes whatever is received when collateral or proceeds are sold, exchanged, collected, or otherwise disposed of.

        1. Security interest in proceeds is continuously perfected if the interest in the original collateral was perfected, but it ceases to be perfected ten days after receipt by the debtor unless a filed financing statement covers the original collateral and the proceeds are similar collateral, the proceeds are identifiable cash proceeds, or the security interest in proceeds is perfected within the ten day period.

VIII. Indispensable paper.

    A. Chattel paper: A writing or writings which evidence both a monetary obligation and a security interest in or a lease of specific goods.

        1. Security interest perfected by filing or by physical possession.

2. A purchaser of chattel paper who gives new value and takes possession of it in the ordinary course of his or her business and without knowledge that the specific paper is subject to a security interest has priority over a security interest which was previously perfected; and if it is chattel paper which is claimed merely as proceeds of inventory subject to a security interest, the purchaser has priority even though he or she knows that the specific paper is subject to the security interest.

B. Instruments: Negotiable instruments, stocks, bonds, and other investment securities.

   1. Perfected by taking physical possession. Two exceptions:

     a. Perfected without taking possession for a period of twenty-one days from the time it attaches to the extent that it arises for new value given under a written security agreement.

     b. If perfected by possession, continues for twenty-one days where the secured party delivers it to the debtor for sale, exchange, presentation, collection, renewal, or registration of transfer.

   2. The two exceptions do not apply to a holder in due course of a negotiable instrument or bona fide purchaser of a security.

C. Documents: Negotiable and nonnegotiable bills of lading and warehouse receipts.

   1. A security interest in goods represented by a negotiable document is perfected by perfecting an interest in the document, by either filing or taking possession of the document. (The two exceptions mentioned in Part B above concerning instruments also apply to negotiable documents.)

   2. Perfection will not give priority over a bona fide purchaser to whom the document has been duly negotiated.

   3. If a bailee in possession of the goods has not issued a negotiable document, then a security interest in the goods is perfected by the issuance of a document in the name of the secured party, by notifying the bailee of the secured party's interest, or by filing as to the goods.

IX. Intangible collateral.

A. Accounts: A right to payment for goods sold or leased or

for services rendered which is not evidenced by an instrument or chattel paper. Perfected by filing.
B. Contract right: Any right to payment under a contract not
yet earned by performance and not evidenced by an instrument or chattel paper. Perfected by filing.
C. General intangibles: Any personal property other than
goods, accounts, contract rights, chattel paper, documents, and instruments. Perfected by filing.

X. Priorities. In addition to the priorities previously mentioned,
the following rules apply:

A. A purchase money security interest in inventory has priority over a conflicting security interest if:
1. The purchase money interest was perfected when the
debtor received the collateral,
2. The purchase money secured party notified prior
secured parties who had filed or were otherwise known
to the party that the financing was to take place before
the debtor received the collateral, and
3. The notice stated that a purchase money security interest was about to be acquired, describing the inventory by item or type.
B. A purchase money security interest in collateral other than
inventory has priority over a conflicting security interest in
the same collateral if the purchase money security interest
is perfected at the time the debtor receives possession of
the collateral or within ten days thereafter.
C. In all other cases, priorities shall be determined as follows:
1. In the order of filing or perfection, whichever occurs
first, regardless of which security interest attached first
or whether it attached before or after filing.
2. In the order of attachment, if none of the security interests are perfected.

XI. Default by debtor. Secured party may:

A. Reduce the claim to judgment or foreclose or otherwise enforce the security interest.
B. May notify an account debtor or obligor to make payment
to him or her.
C. Take possession of collateral without judicial process, if
this can be done without breach of the peace.
D. Sell, lease, or otherwise dispose of collateral.

1. Public or private sale.
2. Debtor entitled to reasonable notice, except in case of:
   a. Perishable goods.
   b. Threat of speedily declining value.
   c. Recognized market.
3. Secured party must account for surplus; debtor liable for deficiency.

E. If the debtor has paid 60 percent of the security interest obligation on consumer goods, the secured party in possession must dispose of the collateral within ninety days.

F. In any other case, the secured party in possession may propose to retain the collateral in satisfaction of the obligation by giving written notice to the parties in interest. If any party in interest objects in writing within twenty-one days, the secured party must dispose of the collateral.

PART TEN
Bankruptcy

Instituting Bankruptcy Proceedings

45

I. Constitution of the United States provides for bankruptcy laws.

    A. Purpose of bankruptcy.
       1. To effect an equitable distribution of the debtor's property among the debtor's creditors.
       2. To relieve honest debtors of hopeless situations in order that they may start afresh, free of their former obligations.

    B. The Bankruptcy Act passed in 1898, amended by the Chandler Act of 1938, was the law until 1979. The Bankruptcy Reform Act of 1978, to take effect October 1, 1979, replaced prior legislation.
       1. The purpose of the new law is to modernize the bankruptcy law and facilitate its administration.
       2. The new law creates in each judicial district a United States bankruptcy court to be an adjunct to the district court for that district.

    C. The United States bankruptcy courts have exclusive jurisdiction over all bankruptcy matters.

II. Structure of the Bankruptcy Act.

    A. Cases are filed in one of four operative chapters: Chapter 7, Liquidation; Chapter 9, Adjustment of Debts of a Municipality; Chapter 11, Reorganization; or Chapter 13, Adjustment of Debts of An Individual With Regular Income.
       1. Cases filed under Chapter 7, Liquidation, are the cases that contemplate total liquidation of the debtor's assets, distribution to creditors, and discharge from remaining liabilities.
       2. The other operative chapters, 9, 11, and 13, contemplate rearrangement and restructuring of the debtor's liabilities under a plan whereby creditors may be paid in full.

    B. Chapter 15, United States Trustees, directs the Attorney General of the United States to appoint one U.S. trustee

for each of ten pilot programs in districts spread throughout the United States.

1. The pilot programs will be under the supervision of an
   assistant attorney general.
2. Each U.S. trustee will establish, maintain, and super-
   vise a panel of private trustees, eligible and available
   to serve as trustees in cases under the Act.
3. Chapter 15 will be repealed automatically as of April 1,
   1984 unless new legislation is enacted.

C. The Judicial Conference of the United States will recommend to the Congress and to the President before May 1,
   1985 and every sixth year thereafter, a uniform percentage
   adjustment of each dollar amount used in the bankruptcy
   law.

III. Liquidation under Chapter 7.

A. Voluntary cases.
   1. Any person, firm, or corporation may file a petition in
      the bankruptcy court for a voluntary case except:
      a. A railroad;
      b. A governmental unit; or
      c. A bank, insurance company, or savings and loan
         association.
   2. Debtor need not be insolvent.
   3. Husband and wife may file a joint case, but this re-
      quires mutual consent.

B. Involuntary cases.
   1. An involuntary case may be commenced against any
      person, firm, or corporation except:
      a. Those that cannot be voluntary cases;
      b. Farmers, individuals who received more than 80
         percent of their gross income in the prior year from
         a farming operation owned and operated by them;
         and
      c. Charitable corporations.
   2. Requirements.
      a. If there are twelve or more creditors, at least three
         must join in filing the petition in the bankruptcy
         court.
      b. If there are less than twelve creditors, one or more
         may file the petition.
      c. Petitioning creditors as a group must own noncon-
         tingent unsecured claims totaling $5,000 or more.
   3. Debtor may file an answer to the petition and ask for a
      trial.

4. Subject to the court's orders, the debtor can continue to operate any business owned, as well as use, acquire or dispose of property until there is an order for relief in the case.

C. Order for relief (adjudication).

1. A voluntary case is commenced by the filing of a petition; commencement of the case constitutes an order for relief.

2. In an involuntary case, the court will issue an order for relief if the debtor does not file an answer to the petition.

3. If the debtor does file an answer, then the court will issue an order for relief after trial, but only if:

   a. The debtor is not paying his debts as they become due; or

   b. Within 120 days before the filing of the petition a receiver was appointed or an assignee under a general assignment for the benefit of the debtor's creditors took possession of the debtor's property.

D. Interim trustee.

1. Promptly after the order for relief, the court appoints an interim trustee to take over the debtor's property.

2. This appointment is terminated upon the election of a permanent trustee.

E. Meetings of creditors.

1. The court calls the first meeting of creditors within a reasonable time after the order for relief.

2. The court may not preside at or attend any meeting of creditors.

3. The debtor must appear and submit to examination by the creditors and the trustee concerning the debtor's assets and other matters which may affect the right of the debtor to obtain a discharge.

4. The creditors may elect a trustee at the meeting of creditors.

5. If the creditors fail to elect a trustee, the interim trustee serves as trustee in the case.

F. Trustee in bankruptcy.

1. Once a trustee is elected or appointed, the trustee is the representative of the debtor's estate, in which capacity the trustee can sue and be sued.

2. Property of the estate is comprised of all legal or equitable interests of the debtor in property as of the commencement of the case, as well as any property acquired by the debtor within 180 days after the petition, through:

   a. Inheritance;

   b. Property settlement agreement with debtor's spouse; or

   c. As beneficiary of a life insurance policy.

  3. It is the trustee's duty to collect all the assets of the debtor, including voidable transfers, and reduce them to cash; approve all claims of creditors; object to debtor's discharge if justified; and otherwise administer the debtor's estate.

 G. Creditors' committee.

  1. The general unsecured creditors may elect a creditors' committee of not less than three nor more than eleven members.

  2. If so elected, this committee may consult with the trustee in connection with the administration of the estate, make recommendations to the trustee respecting the performance of the trustee's duties, and submit to the court any question affecting the administration of the estate.

 H. Utility service.

  1. A utility cannot refuse or discontinue service to the trustee or the debtor solely on the basis that a debt owed by the debtor for service rendered before the order for relief was not paid when due.

  2. A utility may refuse or discontinue service if neither the trustee nor the debtor, within 20 days after the order for relief, furnishes adequate assurance of payment in the form of a deposit or other security.

IV. Debtor's duties and benefits.

 A. Duties.

  1. File a list of creditors, a schedule of assets and liabilities, and a statement of the debtor's financial affairs.

  2. Cooperate with the trustee as necessary to enable the trustee to perform the trustee's duties.

  3. Turn over to the trustee all property of the estate and any books and records relating to such property.

  4. Attend hearings and comply with all lawful orders of the court.

 B. Benefits.

  1. An individual debtor may exempt certain property from the estate by filing a list of the exempt property with the court.

  2. The exempt property is at the debtor's option, either:

a. The property exempt from execution under the law of the state of residence of the debtor; or

b. The property exempted under the Bankruptcy Act.

3. Following are most of the items of property exempt under the Bankruptcy Act:

a. The homestead not exceeding $7,500 in value;

b. A motor vehicle not exceeding $1,200 in value;

c. Household furnishings, wearing apparel, or musical instruments used by the debtor or a dependent of the debtor, not to exceed $200 in value in any particular item;

d. Family jewelry not exceeding $500 in total aggregate value;

e. Any other property up to $400 in total value plus any unused homestead exemption from a. above.

f. Items used in a trade or business not exceeding $750 in total aggregate value;

g. Any unmatured life insurance contract.

4. It is not considered fraudulent for a debtor to convert nonexempt property into exempt property before filing a petition in bankruptcy.

5. The exemptions apply separately to each debtor in a joint case.

6. An individual debtor may redeem consumer goods from a lien securing a dischargeable consumer debt, if the property is exempted under the Bankruptcy Act, by paying the holder of the lien the amount of the secured claim.

46 Administration of Bankruptcy

I. Provable claims.

   A. Provable claims may be filed by a creditor, by the debtor, or by the trustee any time within six months after the first meeting of creditors.

   B. Generally all claims arising prior to the commencement of the case are provable, except:

      1. A claim unenforceable against the debtor, as where the defense of lack of consideration, illegality, fraud, duress, etc. is available;

      2. A claim for unmatured interest. Interest does not accrue after the date of filing a case;

      3. A claim of a landlord for damages resulting from the termination of a lease, to the extent the claim exceeds:

         a. The rent reserved by the lease for the greater of one year, or 15 percent, not to exceed three years, of the remaining term of the lease, plus

         b. Any unpaid rent due under the lease at the time of termination;

      4. A claim for damages resulting from the termination of an employment contract, to the extent the claim exceeds:

         a. The compensation provided by the contract for one year after its termination, plus

         b. The unpaid compensation due under the contract at the time of termination;

   C. A claim of a secured creditor will be allowed to the extent that the claim exceeds the security.

   D. In all cases of mutual debts or mutual credits between the debtor's estate and a creditor, one debt is set off against the other, and the balance only is allowed or paid.

II. Voidable transfers. The trustee has a duty to bring an action to avoid transfers of property of the debtor that are voidable either under the Bankruptcy Act or applicable state law.

III. Voidable preferences.

    A. The trustee can avoid a transfer if five conditions are met:

        1. The transfer was made to or for the benefit of a creditor;

        2. For or on account of an antecedent debt owed by the debtor before the transfer was made;

        3. Made when the debtor was insolvent;

        4. Made during the 90 days preceding the commencement of the case.

            a. If the transfer was to an insider, then it can be avoided if it was made within one year preceding the commencement of the case, if the insider had reasonable cause to believe the debtor was insolvent at the time of the transfer.

            b. An insider is one who has a close relationship with the debtor, such as, a relative or partner of an individual debtor, or an officer, director or person in control of a corporate debtor, or a partner or a relative of a partner in a partnership debtor;

        5. The transfer enabled the creditor to whom or for whose benefit it was made to receive a greater percentage of his or her claim than would have been received under the distributive provisions of the Bankruptcy Act.

    B. The trustee may avoid a transfer of a lien even if the lien has been enforced by sale before the commencement of the case.

    C. Exempted transfers:

        1. Transfers of property for new value given to the debtor;

        2. Transfers made in payment of a debt incurred in the ordinary course of business or financial affairs of the debtor within 45 days after the debt was incurred.

        3. Transfers of purchase money security interests in property.

        4. Payment of a fully secured claim.

    D. There is a rebuttable presumption that the debtor was insolvent during the 90 days preceding the filing of the petition in the case. Insolvency means that the debtor's liabilities exceed his or her assets, at a fair valuation, exclusive of fraudulent transfers and property exempted under the Act.

IV. Fraudulent transfers and obligations.

    A. Types of transfers.

1. A fraudulent transfer or obligation is one made with actual intent to hinder, delay, or defraud a past or future creditor.
2. A transfer is also fraudulent when made for less than a reasonable equivalent consideration and the debtor:
   a. Was or thereby becomes insolvent;
   b. Was engaged in business with an unreasonably small capital; or
   c. Intended to incur debts that would be beyond the debtor's ability to repay.

B. Under federal law, a fraudulent transfer or obligation may be set aside by the trustee if it was made or incurred within one year of the filing of the petition.

C. State law also recognizes fraudulent conveyances. Depending upon the particular state, a fraudulent conveyance may be set aside by the trustee if it was made within the range of two to five years before the filing of the petition.

D. Any other grounds the debtor could have used, such as fraud, mutual mistake, lack of capacity, etc., may be used by the trustee to obtain return of property.

V. Order of priority upon distribution. Each ranked priority must be paid in full before the next ranked priority is paid. There are no priorities within a priority class.

A. Costs and expenses of administering and preserving the estate.

B. Expenses arising in the ordinary course of the debtor's business or financial affairs after a bankruptcy proceeding has been commenced but before the trustee has been appointed.

C. Claims for wages earned by an individual within 90 days before the filing of the petition, up to $2,000 per employee.

D. Claims for unpaid contributions to employee benefit plans arising within 180 days before the filing of the petition, up to $2,000 per employee, reduced by the wage claim in the next preceding priority class.

E. Claims for deposits made for consumer goods or services never received, up to $900 per individual.

F. Claims of governmental units, primarily taxes which became due and owing within three years of filing the petition.

G. Claims of general creditors, including any claims not within the limitations of the above priorities.

H. Anything remaining is paid to the debtor.

VI. Discharge.

    A. Only an individual can be granted a discharge from most of his or her debts under Chapter 7. Hearings on discharge are held if objections to discharge are filed by the trustee or a creditor.

    B. A discharge may be denied for any one of the following reasons:

        1. The debtor is not an individual;

        2. The debtor has made a fraudulent conveyance within one year of the filing of the petition;

        3. The debtor has destroyed, concealed, mutilated, falsified, or failed to keep or preserve any books and records from which the debtor's financial condition might be ascertained, unless the act or failure to act was justified under all the circumstances of the case;

        4. Commission of a bankruptcy crime, such as making a false oath or account, the use or presentation of a false claim, bribery, or withholding from an officer of the estate any recorded information relating to the debtor's property or financial affairs;

        5. The debtor has failed to explain satisfactorily any loss of assets or deficiency of assets to meet the debtor's liabilities;

        6. The debtor has refused to obey any lawful order or answer any material question approved by the court;

        7. The debtor has committed any of the above acts within one year before the filing of the petition in connection with another case concerning an insider;

        8. The debtor has been granted a discharge within six years of filing the petition in the present case;

        9. Approval by the court of a waiver of discharge executed by the debtor.

    C. A discharge can be revoked at the request of the trustee or a creditor within one year after the discharge was granted by showing:

        1. The debtor obtained the discharge through fraud unknown by the requesting party until after the discharge;

        2. The debtor acquired property belonging to the estate, but fraudulently failed to report it to the trustee; or

        3. The debtor refused to testify or obey any lawful order of the court.

VII. Claims not affected by discharge.

    A. Claims for taxes due any political unit.

B. A debt for obtaining money, property, services, or a refinancing extension or renewal of credit by false pretenses, a false representation, or actual fraud, or by use of a statement in writing respecting the debtor's financial condition that is materially false, or on which the creditor reasonably relied, and which the debtor made with intent to deceive.

C. Claims not scheduled in time for proof and allowance, known to the debtor, unless the creditor had notice or actual knowledge of the case in time for proper filing.

D. A claim against the debtor for embezzlement or larceny and a debt for fraud or defalcation of the debtor while acting in a fiduciary capacity.

E. Alimony and child support.

F. Liability resulting from willful and malicious torts.

G. Most liabilities for a fine, penalty, or forfeiture payable to a governmental unit.

H. Student loans, unless such loans have been due and owing for five years or more.

I. Claims that were or could have been scheduled in a prior case in which the debtor waived discharge or a discharge was denied.

VIII. Reaffirmation of a dischargeable debt.

A. Any reaffirmation agreement must be made before the granting of a discharge.

B. May be rescinded by the debtor within thirty days after it becomes enforceable.

C. Individual debtors must have affirmation agreement approved by the court.

D. At discharge hearing the court must:
   1. Advise debtor that affirmations are not legally required, and
   2. Explain to the debtor the legal consequences of the affirmation agreement.

E. Affirmation agreements entered into after discharge are unenforceable.

Other Forms of 47
Relief under the
Bankruptcy Act

I. Reorganization under Chapter 11.

A. Primarily available for businesses, although individuals are eligible. Purpose is to permit debtors to adjust their liabilities, satisfy or modify liens on property, and avoid a liquidation case.
   1. Going concern value of business may be preserved.
   2. Creditors may realize more than in a liquidation case.
   3. Avoids expensive equity receiverships under state law.
   4. Restricts the power of dissenters and makes them less troublesome.

B. A railroad and anyone that can be a debtor in a liquidation case under Chapter 7, except a stockbroker or a commodity broker, may be a debtor in a reorganization under Chapter 11.

C. The proceeding can be either voluntary or involuntary and the same rules apply here as apply to liquidation cases under Chapter 7.

D. Creditors' committees.
   1. After the court issues the order for relief, the court appoints one or more creditors' committees and stockholders' committees to represent the interests of the various types of creditors and stockholders.
   2. These committees consult with the trustee or debtor in possession concerning the administration of the case, investigate the financial activities of the debtor, participate in the formulation of a plan of reorganization, may request the appointment of a trustee or examiner if not previously appointed, and perform such other services in the interest of the group they represent.

E. Appointment of trustee or examiner.
   1. At any time after the commencement of the case, on request of a party in interest, the court may appoint a trustee to take over the estate of the debtor. Otherwise, the debtor remains in possession.

2. If a trustee is not appointed, then the court may appoint an examiner to conduct investigations of the debtor as are appropriate.
3. Duties of trustee.
   a. All of the duties that a trustee has under a liquidation case.
   b. If the debtor has not done so, file with the court the list of creditors, schedule of assets and liabilities, and a statement of affairs.
   c. Investigate the financial activities of the debtor and the desirability of continuance of the business.
   d. File a report of any investigation made of the debtor's affairs with the court and a copy with any creditors' or stockholders' committee.
   e. File a plan of reorganization or a report why no plan is being filed, or recommend conversion of the case to liquidation under Chapter 7 or an adjustment of debts under Chapter 13.
4. Duties of examiner are the same investigative duties a trustee has under c and d above.

F. Debtor in possession. Where no trustee is appointed, the debtor in possession has all the rights, powers, and duties of a trustee, except the investigation duties of a trustee, which may be performed by an examiner, if appointed.

II. The plan.

A. Who may file a plan.
   1. A debtor in possession has exclusive right to file a plan during the first 120 days after the date of the order for relief.
   2. Any party in interest, including the debtor, the trustee or a creditors' or stockholders' committee, may file a plan if:
      a. A trustee has been appointed;
      b. The debtor has not met the 120 day deadline; or
      c. The debtor's plan has not been accepted within 180 days after the date of the order for relief, by each class of creditors whose claims are impaired under the plan.

B. Classification of claims. Classification is based on the nature of the claims or interests classified, and permits inclusion of claims or interests in a particular class only if the claim or interest being included is substantially similar to the other claims or interests of the class.

C. Contents of plan.
1. Designate classes of claims and interests.
2. Specify any class of claims or interests that are not impaired under the plan.
3. Specify the treatment of any class of claims or interests that is impaired under the plan.
4. Provide the same treatment for each claim or interest of a particular class.
5. Provide adequate means for the plan's execution, such as:
   a. Retention by the debtor of all or any part of the property of the estate;
   b. Transfer all or any part of the property of the estate to one or more other entities;
   c. Merge or consolidate;
   d. Sell and distribute all or any of the property of the estate;
   e. Satisfy or modify any lien;
   f. Extend maturity dates or change interest rates of securities;
   g. Issue new securities.
6. Plan cannot provide for the issuance of nonvoting shares and if shares are issued, must provide for appropriate distribution of voting power among the various classes of shares.
D. Acceptance of plan.
1. Adequate information must be given to the holders of claims and interests so that they can make a sound decision in accepting or rejecting the plan.
2. A class of creditors has accepted a plan if at least two-thirds in amount and more than one-half in number of the allowed claims of the class that are voted are cast in favor of the plan.
3. A class of shareholders has accepted a plan if at least two-thirds of the shares of the class are cast in favor of the plan.
4. No acceptances of a plan are required from any class whose claims or interests are unimpaired under the plan.
E. Confirmation of plan.
1. After a hearing on confirmation, the court may confirm a plan if it conforms to all of the requirements as set forth in the Bankruptcy Act, and the court finds it fair and reasonable.
2. Even though a class of claims or interests has not accepted a plan, the court may confirm the plan if it does

not discriminate unfairly, and is fair and equitable, with respect to each class of claims or interests impaired under the plan.

F.   Effect of confirmation.

1.   Plan becomes binding upon all the parties involved.

2.   Debtor is discharged from all claims and interests not provided for under the plan.

III.   Conversion or dismissal.

A.   Debtor may convert a reorganization case under Chapter 11 to a liquidation case under Chapter 7 if:

1.   The debtor is a debtor in possession;

2.   The case is a voluntary case originally commenced as a reorganization case; or

3.   The case had been converted to a reorganization case at the debtor's request.

B.   The court can convert a reorganization case under Chapter 11 to a liquidation case under Chapter 7 or dismiss the case for cause, whichever is in the best interests of creditors and the estate, including:

1.   Absence of a reasonable likelihood of rehabilitation;

2.   Failure to propose a plan;

3.   Denial of confirmation of the plan; or

4.   Inability to consummate the plan.

IV.   Adjustment of debts of an individual with regular income under Chapter 13.

A.   Purpose is to allow individuals with regular income, including debtors engaged in business as well as wage earners, to adjust their debts and make repayment out of future income.

1.   Debtor must be an individual.

2.   Both secured and unsecured debts may be adjusted.

3.   Debtor's unsecured debts must be less than $100,000 and the debtor's secured debts must be less than $350,000.

B.   The court appoints a trustee to carry out the same duties a trustee has in a liquidation case under Chapter 7, and if the debtor is engaged in business, the trustee has the investigative duties a trustee has in a reorganization case under Chapter 11.

C.   The debtor files a plan.

1.   The plan must provide for:

a.   Submission of future income to the trustee sufficient to execute the plan;

    b. Full payment of all claims entitled to priority as in a liquidation case;

    c. Same treatment of each claim in a class;

    d. Modify the rights of both secured and unsecured creditors;

    e. Provide for the curing or waiving of any default on debts.

  2. The plan may not provide for payments over a period that is longer than three years, unless the court, for cause, approves a longer period, but in no case more than five years.

D. Confirmation of plan.

  1. The court will confirm the plan if the plan is fair and reasonable, in the best interests of the creditors, and it appears the debtor will be able to make all payments under the plan.

  2. Confirmation of the plan binds the debtor and all creditors, whether or not they approve the plan.

E. Discharge.

  1. The court will grant a discharge to the debtor after payment has been made of all debts provided for in the plan except debts that are not dischargeable in a liquidation case.

  2. Any time after confirmation of the plan the court may grant a discharge to the debtor before all payments under the plan have been made, if:

    a. Debtor is unable to make all payments because of circumstances beyond the control of the debtor;

    b. The unsecured creditors have received as much as they would have received in a liquidation case; and

    c. Modification of the plan is not practicable.

PART ELEVEN
Real Property and Mortgages

I. Estates of inheritance.

   A. Estates in fee simple.
     1. Highest degree of ownership.
       a. A grant to a person and his or her heirs forever.
       b. Inherent right of alienation and transference to heirs.
       c. Exists even if mortgage is on property.
     2. Limitations on fee simple.
       a. Use and enjoyment subject to being compatible with social objectives.
       b. Subject to eminent domain, police power, and taxation.
       c. Subject to rights of creditors.
       d. Disposition limited by rights of dower and curtesy, if statutes so provide.
       e. Subservient to easements.
       f. Restrictive covenants.

   B. Fees in expectancy (future interests).
     1. A right to a fee simple after the death of life tenant.
     2. Reversion: Created by granting a life estate in another. Fee simple reverts to grantor.
     3. Remainder: Created by granting a life estate in another with provision for fee simple to pass to third person upon death of life tenant.
       a. Vested remainder: Absolute right to fee simple upon termination of life estate.
       b. Contingent remainder: Right to fee simple after termination of life estate is subject to conditions.

   C. Conditional estates and terminable fees. Grantor may provide that:
     1. Right to an absolute estate may be contingent upon the performance of a condition precedent.
     2. Estate may be terminated upon the breach of a condition.
     3. Fee may be terminated if specified use is discontinued.

II.   Life estates.

    A.   Possessory interest for the life of some person or persons.

    B.   Created by:
        1.   Grant or will,
        2.   Dower, curtesy, and/or homestead laws, where statutes so provide.

    C.   Rights of life tenant.
        1.   Ownership may be assigned or mortgaged.
        2.   Life tenant is entitled to income and profits and may work and exhaust resources exploited at time of vesting, but not those not in evidence at the time of vesting.
        3.   Life tenant is bound to preserve the premises for the holder of the remainder or the reversion.

III.   Easements.

    A.   Typical easement rights: Right of way, common driveways, right to lay pipes and erect power lines, use common party walls. Right may not be expanded unilaterally.

    B.   An interest in land: Must comply with Statute of Frauds unless created by law.

    C.   Dominant tenement: Estate which has the benefit and enjoyment of the easement. Servient tenement: Estate subject to the easement.

    D.   Two classes:
        1.   Easement appurtenant: Belongs to, is used by, and follows title of adjoining land.
        2.   Easement in gross: Personal to grantee of easement and not related to adjoining land ownership or use.

    E.   Creation.
        1.   Express: By grant or reservation.
        2.   Implied.
            a.   Usually by necessity from surrounding circumstances (need of ingress and egress implies right of way).
            b.   Occasionally by apparent and permanent use, e.g., common driveway, where not created by mutual express easements.
        3.   Prescription.
            a.   Use must be open and notorious.
            b.   Must be continuous for statutory period and adverse to true owner.
            c.   By statute, in some states, mere use of a way over uninclosed land is presumed to be permissive and not adverse.

IV. Co-ownership.

    A. Undivided ownership interests in the whole of the property.

    B. Joint tenancy.
        1. Grant "to A and B, as joint tenants."
        2. Property passes to surviving tenant upon death of either joint tenant free of debts of deceased.
        3. Four *unities* must be present.
            a. Time: Tenants' interests must vest at same time.
            b. Title: Single conveyance granting all interests.
            c. Interest: Identical interests granted.
            d. Possession: All have same rights of possession.
        4. Can be severed unilaterally by any one of the joint tenants.

    C. Tenancy in common.
        1. Grant "to A and B."
        2. No right of survivorship; deceased tenant's interest passes to his or her heirs.

    D. Tenancy by the entirety. Abolished in some states.
        1. Co-ownership between husband and wife with right of survivorship.
        2. Cannot be severed unless both consent.

    E. Community property. Form of ownership in some states.
        1. All property owned by either spouse before marriage and acquired afterwards by gift or inheritance and rents and profits therefrom are separate property.
        2. All other property, real and personal, acquired after marriage by either spouse or both is community property.
        3. Husband has the right to manage and control the property but may not dispose of property without written consent of wife.
        4. On death of either spouse, one-half of property is subject to testamentary disposition of the decedent. If no will, all to surviving spouse.

V. Transfer of title to real property.

    A. Voluntary transfer.
        1. Public grant.
            a. Title obtained from the government.
            b. Letters of patent issued.
            c. Method of disposing of public lands—homestead laws: Private persons permitted to occupy and develop land; after specified period and payment of fee, title conveyed.

2. Sale or gift.
   a. Transfer accomplished by execution of deed.
   b. Warranty deed: Grantor warrants that he or she has title in fee simple and right to convey, that property is free from encumbrances, and that he or she will defend title. Passes any after-acquired interest of the grantor.
   c. Special warranty deed: Grantor warrants only against defects in title arising while he or she held ownership.
   d. Quitclaim deed: Grantor quits or gives up interest in the property without warranting that he or she has any interest. Used mainly to clear clouds from record titles. Passes only interest grantor had at that time.

B. Involuntary transfer.
   1. Adverse possession.
      a. Must be actual, visible, exclusive, hostile, and continuous for statutory period.
      b. Length of time required to establish title may vary, depending upon whether or not possession is under a recorded conveyance.
      c. Time of adverse possession of one person may be tacked on to the time of another possessor, providing the latter did not wrongfully dispossess the former.
   2. Eminent domain.
      a. Right of government to take property for public use.
      b. United States Constitution, Fifth Amendment: "Nor shall private property be taken for public use without just compensation."
      c. Condemnation proceeding: Owner entitled to due process on question of fair market value.
   3. Transfer resulting from litigation.
      a. Actions of specific performance: Enforcement of real estate sales agreements.
      b. Executions: Real estate sold to satisfy judgments against owner.
      c. Partition actions: Court severs interests of co-owners. Division in kind favored, but sale and division of proceeds usually necessary.
      d. Quiet title actions: Interests of persons who might have claims on property terminated.
      e. Foreclosures: Equity of owner terminated for failure to fulfill mortgage obligations.

   f. Bankruptcy: Nonexempt real estate becomes part of bankrupt estate.

 C. Survivorship, will, or descent.

  1. Survivorship.

   a. Title to real property held in joint tenancy passes to survivor free from rights of decedent's creditors.

   b. Transfer is subject to mortgages and taxes, if any.

   c. Court proceeding may be necessary.

  2. Will.

   a. Except for property held in joint tenancy and dower and curtesy interests of the spouses, where statutes so provide, title to real property may be passed by will.

   b. Except for rare cases of mutual wills, devise of real property in will has no significance until death.

  3. Descent: Statutory provision for disposition of solely owned real property of decedents where there is no will.

 D. Accretion.

  1. Gradual accumulation of land by action of water.

  2. Applies to land adjoining waters; riparian owners.

VI. The real estate transaction.

 A. Preliminary contract.

  1. Statute of Frauds requires a memorandum.

  2. Usually, buyer makes offer to purchase which is subsequently accepted by seller.

  3. Common provisions.

   a. Names of parties, description of property (may be simply street address), price and prorations, and date and place of closing.

   b. Deposit in escrow (held by third party).

   c. Transaction may be made subject to buyer's ability to obtain financing.

   d. What to pass with land.

   e. Seller to present evidence of merchantable title.

 B. Evidence of title.

  1. Abstract.

   a. Consists of significant portions of all recorded instruments affecting property. Abstract company liable if negligent.

   b. Legal opinion desirable as to whether or not title is merchantable based on examination of abstract.

   c. Examiner follows chain of title and looks for:

    (1) Misdescriptions, discrepancies in names.

        (2)   Improperly executed deeds, unreleased or improperly released mortgages.

        (3)   Failure of spouse to join in conveyances.

        (4)   Restrictions limiting use of property.

        (5)   Judgments, mechanic's liens, and tax liens.

        (6)   Improper legal proceedings.

    d.   Opinion is not insurance, but examiner liable if negligent.

2.   Title insurance.

    a.   Used in place of abstract and opinion.

    b.   Excludes from coverage matters to which the title company has excepted.

    c.   May, by its terms, be limited to matters of record and not cover matters of record since commitment.

3.   Seller has duty of correcting objections which make title unmerchantable.

C.   Closing.

1.   Date is not of the essence, but unreasonable delay may give rise to damages.

2.   Documents.

    a.   Deed, executed as required by statute.

    b.   Real estate transfer fee, if any.

    c.   Seller's statement, showing credits to parties.

    d.   Affidavit as to mechanic's liens: No potential claims for work done on property.

3.   Recording of deed.

D.   Land contract financing.

1.   Usually used where buyer has only nominal down payment and financing is not available from third party.

2.   Title does not pass until payment is complete. Buyer has equitable title with essentially same responsibility as if he or she held legal title.

3.   Strict foreclosure in event of default. Purchaser is allowed a reasonable period in which to redeem, depending on how much has been paid in, after which seller is entitled to writ of assistance.

E.   Mortgage financing.

1.   Buyer obtains legal title upon closing.

2.   Buyer executes mortgage to seller or third person.

Real Estate Mortgages 49

I. Nature of a mortgage.

    A. A mortgage is a conveyance of a security interest in land to secure payment of a debt.

        1. In title theory states, a mortgage is an absolute conveyance of title to the mortgagee, upon condition that the title will revert back to the mortgagor upon payment of the debt.

            a. Mortgagee has immediate right to possession of the land.

            b. Mortgagee has immediate right to collect future rents and profits of the land.

        2. In lien theory states, a mortgage does not convey title but grants to the creditor a mortgagee's lien on the land to secure the debt.

            a. The mortgagor retains legal title and with it the right to posses and use the land.

            b. Right of possession remains in the mortgagor even after default until the mortgage foreclosure is completed.

    B. The mortgage papers.

        1. The mortgage is the document that creates the security interest in the land.

            a. It should be recorded immediately so that anyone subsequently acquiring an interest in the land will do so subject to the mortgagee's rights.

            b. A mortgage drawn to cover after acquired property creates a lien at the time the property is acquired.

            c. A deed absolute on its face will be treated as a mortgage if parol evidence indicates the parties used the deed for the purpose of securing a loan.

        2. The mortage note represents the debt secured by the mortgage.

            a. The note can be negotiable or nonnegotiable.

            b. The mortgage does not create a lien until consideration is actually given for the notes.

            c. The mortgage note is not recorded.

II. Rights and duties of the mortgagor.

 A. The mortgagor may lease, sell, give away, or transfer by
     will his or her interest in the property subject only to the
     claim of the mortgage.
     1. Dower may exist in the mortgagor's interest, where
         statutes so provide.
     2. The mortgagor's interest is subject to execution by his
         or her judgment creditors.
     3. A mortgage executed subsequent to a lease is junior to
         the rights of the tenant under the lease.
     4. A lease executed subsequent to a mortgage will not
         bind the mortgagee.
 B. The mortgagor can convey the land by deed to a subse-
     quent purchaser.
     1. Purchaser who buys the property subject to the
         mortgage is not personally liable for the mortgage.
     2. Purchaser is personally liable for the mortgage debt if
         the deed recites that he or she "assumes and agrees to
         pay" the debt. Mortgagee becomes a third party ben-
         eficiary under the deed.
     3. In any event, the mortgagor is still personally liable on
         the debt.
         a. If purchaser assumes the debt, mortgagor then be-
             comes a surety on the debt.
         b. Mortgagor can be released if a novation is entered
             into.

III. Rights and duties of the mortgagee.

 A. Mortgagee is entitled to repayment of the debt and, if
     mortgagor defaults, may foreclose the mortgage.
     1. Default of one payment on an installment note does
         not allow foreclosure on the full debt unless there is an
         acceleration clause in the mortgage note.
     2. The mortgagee is not obligated to accept payments on
         the debt before they are due unless there is a pre-
         payment clause in the mortgage note.
 B. The mortgagee has the right to protect his or her security
     for the debt.
     1. The mortgagor cannot commit waste on the property.
     2. If mortgagor does not pay the taxes on the property or
         does not insure the property as agreed, the mortgagee
         can pay these items and add them to the mortgage
         debt.
 C. The mortgagee can assign the mortgage and the mortgage
     debt.

1. If mortgagee transfers the note without assignment of the mortgage, the transferee is still entitled to the benefit of the mortgage, for the security follows the debt.
2. Assignment of mortgage should be recorded immediately in order to protect rights of assignee against third persons dealing with the assignor.
3. If note is nonnegotiable, assignee must give actual notice of the assignment to the mortgagor, otherwise an innocent mortgagor's payment of the debt to the assignor would discharge the debt.
4. If note is negotiable, the burden is on the mortgagor to pay the holder of the note in any event.

D. Once the mortgage debt has been paid in full, the mortgagee is obligated to give the mortgagor a release or mortgage satisfaction, which is recorded in order to clear the mortgage from the chain of title.

IV. Mortgagor's equity of redemption.

A. At any time after default in payment of the note and before foreclosure, the mortgagor has the right to redeem the property by paying off the total debt, interest, and any costs incurred by the mortgagee.

B. In many states, even after foreclosure the mortgagor has the right to redeem the property within a specified period of time, usually one year.

V. Foreclosure upon default by mortgagor.

A. Strict foreclosure.
1. The mortgagee gets the property free from the right of redemption after the date specified in the foreclosure decree.
2. Not permitted in most states.

B. Foreclosure by judicial sale.
1. Judgment of foreclosure is entered.
2. Property is sold by court official at public auction. Mortgagee may bid at the sale.
3. Proceeds of sale are used to pay off the mortgage debt and other costs; excess is paid over to the mortgagor.
4. If property does not sell for enough to pay off mortgage debt, mortgagee may obtain a deficiency judgment against the mortgagor.

C. Foreclosure by exercise of power of sale.
1. In many states, if the mortgage grants a power of sale to the mortgagee, he or she can sell the property at public auction without a judicial proceeding.

    2.   Generally the mortgagee cannot bid at such sale.

    3.   If mortgagee is not paid in full, he or she may get a deficiency judgment.

VI.   Special types of mortgages.

   A. Purchase money mortgage.
      1.   Mortgage given by buyer on land purchased to secure loan used to pay part or all of purchase price.
      2.   May be given to the seller or to a third party lender.
      3.   A purchase money mortgage has priority over all other outside claims against the mortgagor-purchaser.
      4.   In some jurisdictions mortgagee cannot get a deficiency judgment upon foreclosure of a purchase money mortgage.

   B. Future advance or open end mortgage.
      1.   A mortgage given for present value which provides that it will also secure an advance of money to be made later.
      2.   The security behind each advance dates back to the date of the mortgage and has priority over any intervening liens of the property.
      3.   If the promise to repay future advances is not made at the time the mortgage is first given but is made at a later time when an advance is made, it is ineffective, and the subsequent advance will not be secured by the mortgage.

   C. Trust deed mortgage.
      1.   A trust deed conveys the property to a third person as trustee for the benefit of the creditors.
      2.   The trustee issues notes to the creditors for the money they lend.
      3.   Advantage is that several notes can be secured by the one trust deed, the notes being easily negotiated without subsequent assignments of the mortgage.
      4.   Foreclosed the same as a regular mortgage.

Landlord and Tenant 50

I. Creation of a leasehold estate.

A. A lease is a contract by which the owner of an estate in land, the landlord or lessor, grants to the tenant or lessee, an exclusive right to use and possess the land for a definite or ascertainable period of time or term.

B. The grant of the possessory term to the tenant is an estate in land, the landlord retaining a reversionary interest.

C. A lease for a term longer than one year must be in writing in order to be enforceable. In some jurisdictions the writing requirement applies only to leases of more than three years duration.

II. Rights and duties of the landlord.

A. At common law, the landlord must give the tenant a right of possession at the inception of the lease.

1. Under majority rule, landlord is not required to deliver physical possession to the tenant.

2. Landlord must bring action to evict someone else wrongfully in possession, but new tenant is not relieved of the obligation to pay rent from the inception of the lease.

3. Tenant can guard against this by an appropriate provision in the lease.

B. Landlord's implied covenant of quiet and peaceful enjoyment.

1. If the tenant is wrongfully evicted by the landlord or evicted by someone having better title than the landlord, the tenant's obligations under the lease are terminated.

2. Doctrine of constructive eviction.

a. Where landlord has done anything which causes a substantial and lasting injury to the tenant's beneficial enjoyment of the premises, the tenant may terminate the lease.

223

      b.   Tenant must abandon possession in order to claim constructive eviction.

      c.   The landlord is not responsible for the wrongful acts of third parties.

C. Landlord's duty to maintain, repair, or restore the premises.

    1. There is no implied warranty that the premises are fit for the purposes for which they are leased.

      a.   Some jurisdictions hold otherwise.

      b.   Exception to this rule is furnished apartment, which landlord must maintain in a tenantable condition.

      c.   State zoning ordinances and health and safety regulations may also impose certain duties upon the landlord.

    2. Landlord has no duty to repair the premises.

      a.   Changed by statute in some states.

      b.   Must maintain and repair any portions of the premises which remain under his or her control.

    3. Landlord has no duty to rebuild upon destruction of the premises by fire or other fortuitous cause.

    4. By express provisions in the lease, the landlord can assume any of the obligations mentioned above.

      a.   Such provisions will be treated as independent covenants, breach of which gives rise to an action for damages only.

      b.   Upon breach, tenant still liable for rent.

      c.   Upon breach, tenant cannot terminate lease unless breach constituted constructive eviction or unless lease provision gave right of termination upon breach.

III.   Rights and duties of the tenant.

A. Tenant's obligation to pay rent.

    1. At common law, there is an implied covenant that the tenant is obligated to pay reasonable rent, the rent being payable only at the end of the term.

    2. Practically all leases have an express covenant by the tenant to pay rent in stated installments and/or in advance.

    3. At common law, unless the lease so provides, nonpayment of rent does not terminate the lease; the only remedy of the landlord is an action for breach of contract.

4. In most states, statutes provide that the landlord can evict the tenant for nonpayment of rent.

5. If the landlord evicts the tenant for nonpayment of rent or breach of any other covenant in the lease pursuant to an express provision in the lease or under a statute, the lease is terminated.

   a. The tenant is relieved of any further payment of rent unless

   b. The lease has a *survival clause* providing that the eviction will not relieve tenant of liability for damages measured by the difference between the rent reserved and the rent received upon reletting.

6. A tenant who wrongfully abandons the premises is still liable for rent unless landlord accepts surrender of the leasehold estate.

   a. Acceptance of surrender can be express or implied.

   b. Reentry and attempt to relet by the landlord is acceptance of surrender unless the lease contains a survival clause as described above.

7. At common law, destruction of the premises by fire or other fortuitous cause does not terminate the lease or relieve the tenant of obligation to pay rent.

   a. Rule does not apply if tenant occupies only a portion of a building.

   b. Rule has been modified in many states by statute.

   c. Most leases contain provisions covering this situation, usually giving the landlord the option to repair and restore—payment of rent suspended until restored—or of terminating the lease.

B. Tenant's use of the premises.

   1. Tenant can use the premises in any manner that is reasonable, lawful, and not in conflict with the terms of the lease.

   2. Tenant cannot commit waste on the property.

C. Tenant's duty to repair and improve premises.

   1. The tenant has no duty to make repairs to the premises unless the lease so provides.

   2. The tenant cannot make any structural changes on the premises without the landlord's consent.

   3. Any structural improvements made by the tenant become part of the real estate and revert to the landlord at the termination of the lease.

D. Tenant's right to remove tenant's fixtures.

   1. Must remove tenant's fixtures within the term of the lease.

2. Cannot remove fixtures which are so firmly built into the premises that it will cause serious damage to remove them.

3. Cannot remove replacement fixtures unless the replaced fixture is reinstalled.

IV. Transfers during the term of the lease.

A. Landlord can sell or mortgage premises at any time, subject, however, to the terms of the lease.
1. Tenant who continues to pay rent to original landlord in good faith, however, is protected.
2. When tenant is notified of change of ownership, he or she must pay rent to new owner-landlord.

B. Assignment and subleases.
1. An assignment transfers possession for the entire balance of the term of the lease to another party.
   a. Leases are freely assignable unless restricted by a provision in the lease.
   b. Both lessee and assignee are liable to the landlord for payment of the rent and other provisions in the lease.
   c. Original lessee is not relieved of any liability and is in the position of assignee's surety to the landlord.
2. A sublease transfers something less than the whole leasehold estate held by the lessee to another person.
   a. Lessee can sublet unless restricted by terms in the lease.
   b. Sublessee has no obligation to the landlord.
   c. Original lessee is still fully liable under the lease.

V. Informal rental arrangements.

A. Periodic tenancy.
1. Tenancy where there is no formal lease and the rent is payable at regular intervals such as month to month or year to year.
2. Where there is a lease for a year or more, and the tenant holds over, the landlord has the option to hold the tenant to a periodic tenancy from year to year, unless stated otherwise in the lease.
3. If the lease is for less than a year and the tenant holds over, the landlord has the option to hold the tenant to a periodic tenancy from month to month, unless stated otherwise in the lease.

4. A periodic tenancy is also created when an oral lease is for a year or more and unenforceable because of the Statute of Frauds.

    a. A lessee who has gone into possession of the premises and pays rent periodically becomes a periodic tenant.

    b. All of the other terms of the oral lease are applicable.

B. Tenancy at will: Tenant in possession without any definite agreement for regular payment of rent or a definite period of time.

C. Tenancy at sufferance: Tenant in possession without a valid lease.

VI. Termination of tenancies.

A. A lease for a definite term expires at the end of the term without any notice of termination.

    1. A tenant who holds over is a tenant at sufferance.

    2. Landlord has option of either bringing action to evict tenant or treating tenancy as periodic.

B. A periodic tenancy can be terminated by either landlord or tenant giving proper notice of termination.

    1. The common law requires six months' notice in tenancies from year to year.

        a. Many states have changed this by statute.

        b. The parties can agree otherwise in the lease.

    2. The common law requires notice one rent period in advance for tenancies of less than one year, unless agreed otherwise in the lease or modified by statute.

C. No notice requirement to terminate tenancies at will or at sufferance.

PART TWELVE
Wills, Estates and Trusts

Wills and Decedents' Estates

I. Will, a testamentary disposition of property.

   A. Does not take effect until death.

   B. Can be revoked any time before death.

   C. Testator must have both the power and the capacity to make a will.

      1. The power to make a will is granted by the state, usually to anyone eighteen years of age or older.

      2. A person has mental capacity to make a will who has the ability to understand and comprehend the nature and extent of his or her property, as well as the disposition he or she is making of the property, and to remember his or her relatives.

   D. Formalities of a will.

      1. Must be in writing.

         a. An exception is the nuncupative or oral will.

         b. One can incorporate into a will by reference another document which in itself is not a will if it is:

            (1) In writing.

            (2) In existence when the will is executed.

            (3) Adequately described in the will.

            (4) Described in the will as being in existence.

      2. The will must be signed by the testator.

      3. There must be attestation (witnessing).

         a. Signature of testator must be witnessed by at least two witnesses. Some states require three.

         b. Testator must sign in witnesses' presence, and witnesses must sign in testator's presence and in the presence of each other.

         c. Any necessary witness who is also a beneficiary under the will, can take under the will only that share he or she would be entitled to had there been no will at all. Same rule for spouses of witnesses in some states.

4. The will must be free from undue influence, fraud, or mistake; otherwise it may be set aside.

E. Revocation of a will.

1. By act of the testator.

a. A will is revoked by physical mutilation or alteration of the will by the testator or by someone at his or her request and in his or her presence with intent to revoke.

b. A subsequent will, if so stated or to the extent a later will is inconsistent with an earlier will, revokes the earlier will.

2. By operation of law.

a. A marriage generally revokes a will executed prior to the marriage unless executed in contemplation of marriage.

b. Generally, any provision in a will in favor of a spouse is revoked by divorce.

c. The subsequent birth of a child will not revoke the will, but the child is entitled to the same share as though the testator died without a will unless it appears from the will that the omission was intentional.

3. The surviving spouse has the right to renounce the will and take the share he or she would take had the testator died without a will.

F. Ademption occurs when a testator neglects to change his or her will after changed circumstances have rendered impossible the performance of a provision in the will. If subject matter of specific legacy was disposed of after will was made, beneficiary gets nothing in place of it.

G. Abatement is the proportional reduction of specific cash gifts when funds or assets out of which such gifts are to be made are not sufficient to pay them in full.

II. Special types of wills.

A. Nuncupative will is an oral will:

1. Valid if made during the last sickness of the testator,

2. Made in the presence of witnesses called for that purpose, and

3. Reduced to writing shortly thereafter.

4. Generally, can transfer only personal property.

5. Cannot replace a validly executed written will.

6. Not recognized in all states.

B. Holographic will.

       1. A will written entirely in the handwriting of the testator.

       2. Valid without witnesses.

       3. Not recognized in all states.

  C. Codicil.

       1. An addition to or revision of a will, generally by a separate instrument, in which the will is expressly referred to and, in effect, incorporated by reference into the codicil.

       2. Must be executed like a will.

III. Intestate succession.

  A. The estate of a person who dies without a will passes by intestate succession as provided by state law.

  B. Distribution of property is generally as follows:

       1. If no lineal descendants, all to surviving spouse.

       2. If there are lineal descendants (children, heirs of children) and a surviving spouse, then a specified share to surviving spouse, usually one-third, balance to lineal descendants.

          a. If lineal descendants are not of equal degree of relationship, they take *per stirpes* (by right of representation).

          b. If lineal descendants are of equal degree of relationship, they take *per capita* (share equally).

       3. If there are lineal descendants and no surviving spouse, lineal descendants take all as provided in a and b of item 2 above.

       4. If there are no lineal descendants and no surviving spouse, then estate ascends to testator's ascendants (parents, grandparents, etc.).

       5. If there are no surviving spouse, descendants, or ascendants, then estate passes to collateral relatives, first brothers and sisters and their descendants; second, aunts and uncles and their descendants, and so on.

  C. The only heir under intestate succession who is not a blood relative is the surviving spouse.

IV. Administration of estates.

  A. Whether a person dies leaving a will (testate) or dies without a will (intestate), his or her estate must be probated.

  B. Personal representative is appointed by the court.

       1. Called an executor or executrix if appointed under a will.

2. Called an administrator or administratrix if appointed by the court without a will.
3. Estate is the personal representative's responsibility; he or she must account to the testator's creditors and the beneficiaries of the estate.
4. Personal representative occupies a fiduciary position in the administration of the estate.

C. Steps in probate procedure.
   1. Proof of the will, if any.
   2. Proof of heirship.
   3. Issuance of letters testamentary or letters of administration, establishing authority of personal representative.
   4. Filing of an inventory of the estate.
   5. Publication of notice for creditors to file claims.
   6. Payment of creditors.
   7. Filing of estate and inheritance tax returns, if any.
   8. Distribution to beneficiaries.
   9. Final account.

I.   Nature of a trust.

  A. The legal title to property is held by one person while the right to the use and benefit of the same property is enjoyed by another.

  B. Parties to a trust.

   1. Creator or settlor.
       a. Person creating the trust.
       b. Any person legally capable of making a contract can create a trust.

   2. Trustee.
       a. Person to whom legal title of the trust property is transferred.
       b. Anyone legally capable of dealing with property may be a trustee, including the settlor.
       c. A trustee can decline to serve any time before acceptance.
           (1) Lack of a trustee will not destroy a trust.
           (2) If trustee dies or if nominated trustee declines to serve, court will appoint one.
       d. Duties of trustee.
           (1) To carry out the purposes of the trust.
           (2) To act with prudence and care in the administration of the trust.
           (3) To exercise a high degree of loyalty toward the beneficiary with whom he or she has a fiduciary relationship.
       e. The powers of a trustee are determined by:
           (1) The rules of law in the jurisdiction in which the trust is established.
           (2) The authority granted the trustee by the settlor in the instrument creating the trust.

   3. Beneficiary or *cestui que* trust.
       a. Person who has the right to the use and benefit of the trust property.

       b. Very few restrictions on who (or what) may be a beneficiary.

       c. Trust will fail if there is a lack of an identifiable beneficiary.

       d. Except for a spendthrift trust, creditors can attach the interest of the beneficiary.

       e. Except for a spendthrift trust, beneficiary can assign his or her interest to another.

C. The trust property must be specific, in existence, and capable of being transferred by the settlor at the time the trust is created.

D. Consideration is not necessary in order to create an enforceable trust.

E. Termination of a trust.

    1. Expiration according to the terms of the trust agreement.

    2. Impossibility of performance or supervening illegality of the trust are grounds for judicial termination.

    3. Consent of all the beneficiaries may terminate a trust except for a spendthrift trust, unless the settlor also consents.

    4. Merger of the beneficial interest with the legal title of the trust property in one person will terminate the trust.

F. Rule against perpetuities applies to private trusts. Rule: An interest created in property must become fixed (vested) within a life or lives in being and twenty-one years. Rule modified in some states.

II. Types of trusts.

A. Express trusts.

    1. *Inter vivos* or living trust is one created during the lifetime of the settlor.

    2. Testamentary trust is one created by the settlor's will to become effective only when the will takes effect after his or her death.

    3. Spendthrift trust is one that provides in the trust agreement that the beneficiary cannot, by assignment or otherwise, impair his or her rights to receive principal or income and that creditors of the beneficiary cannot attach the fund or the income.

    4. Charitable trust is one created to serve any public purpose.

       a. Rule against perpetuities does not apply to charitable trusts.

    b. *Cy pres* doctrine, which applies only to charitable trusts, provides that when it is impossible or impracticable to carry out a charitable bequest exactly as directed by the settlor, a court will apply the funds to a charity as similar as possible in purpose to that specified.

B. Trust implied by operation of law.

    1. Constructive trust.

        a. Imposed by law in order to prevent unjust enrichment of a party with title to property which ought to belong to another.

        b. Arises regardless of the intention of the parties.

    2. Resulting trust.

        a. Imposed to carry out the true intent of the parties.

        b. Occurs whenever legal title is transferred to one who is not intended to have the beneficial interest of the property.